HUMANISM IN
PERSONOLOGY

HUMANISM IN PERSONOLOGY
Allport, Maslow, and Murray

SALVATORE R. MADDI
PAUL T. COSTA

AldineTransaction
A Division of Transaction Publishers
New Brunswick (U.S.A.) and London (U.K.)

New paperback printing 2008

Copyright © 1972 by Salvatore R. Maddi and Paul T. Costa, Jr.

This book is printed on acid-free paper that meets the American National Standard for Permanence of Paper for Printed Library Materials.

Library of Congress Catalog Number: 2007031521
ISBN: 978-0-202-36173-4
Printed in the United States of America

Library of Congress Cataloging-in-Publication Data

Maddi, Salvatore R.
  Humanism in personology : Allport, Maslow, and Murray / Salvatore R.
    Maddi and Paul T. Costa.
      p. cm.
  Originally published: c1971.
  Includes bibliographical references and index.
  ISBN 978-0-202-36173-4
    1. Personality. 2. Humanistic psychology. 3. Allport, Gordon W. (Gordon Willard), 1897-1967. 4. Maslow, Abraham H. (Abraham Harold) 5. Murray, Henry Alexander, 1893-1988. I. Costa, Paul T. II. Title.

BF698.M2367 2007
150.19'86--dc22

                                                    2007031521

For Carol and Dorothy

Foreword

Because two of the psychologists whose work is illuminated in this book have died and the third is in partial retirement, students and their teachers may be inclined to treat Allport, Maslow and Murray as historical figures rather than as contemporaries. This would be a great mistake. In their choice of problems, research methods, and, particularly, their definition of the significant issues of individual psychology, they are as fresh as tomorrow. Indeed, these three men were ahead of their time; their concerns were those that will be increasingly voiced in the decades ahead as they were not during the years of their highest productivity.

The authors, Salvatore R. Maddi and Paul T. Costa, because of their respective associations with Harvard University, are able to draw on personal experiences as well as the literature in writing what is, in fact, an appreciation as well as a critical review of theoretical formulations. Moreover, both authors are themselves representative of the kind of psychologist the three theorists would surely have liked to produce in greater numbers—empirical scientists who never lose sight of the fact that participants in their research are complex, functioning individuals. Allport, Maslow and Murray were staunchly independent thinkers who swam resolutely against the prevailing flow of the science of psychology in their time. They identified themselves with problems intrinsically interesting to any intelligent human being at a time when psychology was largely preoccupied with matters too recondite or too dull to create much interest except among initiates. They traveled easily in the company of humanists, speaking their language and drawing inspiration from them while many of their compeers were more comfortable with engineers, mathematicians, and neurophysiologists. Above all, they were perhaps the last major figures in psychology with the effrontery to attempt to construct comprehensive theories of human behavior.

In two recent reviews of texts on concepts of personality, the authors felt constrained to toll the knell of "global" theory. They asserted, as others have, that major theorists will be infrequently or perfunctorily cited in reports of empirical research on personality, restating the frequent criticism that comprehensive theories are so imprecisely stated that no rigorous tests of their propositions can be made.

From the standpoint of the empirical scientist these are just criticisms: it is difficult to operationalize theoretical concepts of personality and even more difficult to achieve a logical articulation of one concept with another. However, it is one thing to offer cogent criticism of a theory and quite another to deny the utility of comprehensive theoretical statements.

What are "global" or "comprehensive" theories and why are they important? Essentially such statements undertake to provide explanatory principles for the full range of consequential human behavior rather than merely one segment or domain. Thus a global theory cannot conveniently ignore questions concerning basic and derivative motivations, mediating structures and control devices. Above all, a comprehensive theory must attempt to take account of the manifest, observable behavior of functioning humans outside the laboratory. The mark of the global theorist is his willingness to set up a scheme sufficiently

flexible and broad in scope so that virtually any significant behavior or sequence of behavior of any individual can be illuminated by its explanatory principles. In this sense, he speaks
more directly to the curious layman than most scientists do.
The global theorist is concerned with both similarities and differences among humans, with both full involvement and ambivalence, with the reconciliation of long-term goals and
intercurrent environmental pressures. Hence, he is likely to be
deeply introspective himself, and concerned with multifaceted
and longitudinal investigations of individuals including as data
their own interpretations of their behavior.

Existing comprehensive theories are important not because
they are fully developed explanations of human behavior, but
because they ask most of the important questions about the
subject in a coherent fashion. Every human being is to some
degree self-questioning. Many individuals, indeed, become
proficient in both self-exploration and observation of others
and are able to articulate some general principles which seem
to govern their own and others' behavior. Readers who have
this talent will be particularly drawn to Allport, Maslow, and
Murray just as the self-taught artist is drawn to the work of
masters. Yet surely even those with little curiosity about themselves will be tempted to pit their "common sense" understanding of human activity against these three experts, for all of
them speak with feeling as well as wisdom to issues that concern all men.

From the inception of psychology in the late 19th century
as a scientific discipline, research has been held in considerably
higher esteem than arcane speculations about the nature of
man, and the shortcomings of a purely empirical approach to
the study of personality have not been given sufficient attention. The intellectual climate in America is particularly recep-
tive to "facts," but the pragmatism and objectivity in which we
take so much pride also make us vulnerable to accepting
answers for which there are no valid questions. The pre-

eminent value of theory is that of defining and ordering the questions which need to be asked: the tentative explanations incorporated in theories need not be taken too seriously as long as the questions they purport to answer are kept in focus.

Because psychology was among the last of the scientific disciplines to leave the parental home—to seek an identity separate and distinct from philosophy—its professors were strongly motivated to mature quickly. To assert independence and gain respectability in the shortest possible time, they adopted a rigorous investigational method designed to enhance a strict objectivity toward the subject matter of psychology. However, by trying to free itself of any vestige of "moral philosophy," psychology largely denied itself what was and still is a potentially highly productive source of data—the human subject construing his own experience.

In retrospect it is a bit puzzling that a discipline interested in individual human behavior did not devote some considerable portion of its efforts to studying and theorizing about just that—intact individuals behaving over their life span in their natural social and physical environment. Almost no one (other than anthropologists whose interests are not primarily psychological) takes any systematic account of what people do when freely behaving, what they have to say about their experience, and how they explain their behavior. The history of most sciences includes a descriptive phase before a formal taxonomy is developed. Breaking up major problems into highly specialized research areas is usually a very late stage in the development of a science—a stage that can most confidently be undertaken in the framework of a widely acceptable, comprehensive theory. Psychology, virtually from its inception as an empirical science, dispersed its investigative efforts over a wide range of specialized areas of inquiry without the benefit of an accepted theoretical framework or set of objectives. There have been countless small areas of inquiry delineated and assiduously pursued. Psychology has never been a unified structure, but a sprawling market place comprising boutiques of every shape and size. Only method has brought a degree of unity to the field, and there are sharp, often irreconcilable differences between advocates of the experimental mode, the multivariate design employing statistical controls, and clinical or observational techniques.

Would contemporary psychology be substantially different if the influential figures in its early history had been less ambitious to attain a position of respect among their colleagues from the older and "harder" sciences? One likes to believe that an initial modesty and naiveté in confronting the data of individual human behavior would have been advantageous over the long run. If psychology had firmly and unequivocally organized itself around the study of the behavior of the intact human being rather than trying to ride piggy-back on the methods and preoccupations of other sciences, we might have lost something in the speed and magnitude of development as an academic and applied profession, but we would have gained more coherence as a science. The intense work on learning, cognition, motivation, perception, sensation, and other standard problems of psychology would have been undertaken with the aim of explicating the behavior of man rather than putatively throwing light on some subassembly of the human species as a laboratory animal.

In recent years there has been a small flurry of interest in naturalistic observation and in learning about human behavior through the study of lives or parts thereof. It is paradoxical that this line of inquiry, which might appropriately have been a first stage in the development of psychology, is gaining attention at this late date—indeed, perhaps too late to exert a broad influence on psychology. The counterthrust of the humanists against the establishment may give such research a certain cachet just as the "discovery" of autonomous ego functions by neopsychoanalytic theorists gave Allport's theory prominence in a somewhat (to him) alien intellectual quarter. But the humanists do not speak for those psychologists who are fully sympathetic with the aims of science but believe the field has chosen the wrong problems to work on. It is paradoxical, is it not, that psychologists, who should be preeminent among scientists in helping to solve obtrusive human problems, have such a faint voice and feeble technology?

But who knows? There is growing interest in applying psychology to the solution of many current social and environmental problems, and those venturesome psychologists who have gone into the field have returned with the news that there is much needed knowledge about human behavior that is hard to deduce either from work in the laboratory or the clinic. They advise learning more about how people see themselves, their options, and the forces impinging upon them before any significant interventions are undertaken. Allport, Maslow and Murray would applaud such wisdom.

The three theorists whose work is described in this volume never let their science come between them and their interest in behaving, intact, self-governing humans, and as a consequence their science was enriched. In theorizing they kept before them their own images as fully functioning, complex, self-examining human beings and they did not permit themselves to assume that any other human was in any unbridgeable way different from themselves. They never lost sight of the target of psychological theory and research: to comprehend individual behavior as it can be observed in behaving intact humans.

If their theories seem incomplete or incorrect in detail in the light of subsequent research, that is only to be expected. For a variety of reasons, some of which have been alluded to above, they did not command their fair share of resources in a discipline that seems often more devoted to method than to its subject matter. The value of their approach to psychology has never been as fully realized as it might have been had the field taken a different view of its mission, with generations of graduate students devoting their talents to shaping a comprehensive theory and challenging it with suitably designed relevant investigations.

Nevertheless, they stand as examples of what psychology might have been under other circumstances and may yet have to become if the science is to realize its promise to mankind.

Ralph W. Heine

Preface

What we hope to do in this book is to illuminate the humanistic emphasis in the study of personality by scrutinizing the general intellectual assumptions, formal theories, research, and personal lives of Allport, Maslow, and Murray. These three psychologists have been chosen because they have been steadfast in their humanistic emphases from the beginnings of their careers nearly four decades ago. It should be instructive to realize that the present flood of interest in humanistic views of the person represents agreement with existing though previously unpopular positions more than the invention of new approaches.

This is not to say that everything in the viewpoints of Allport, Maslow, and Murray has suddenly become popular. They showed a predisposition toward broad, comprehensive, and necessarily complex theorizing not present in contemporary emphases. But such theorizing will surely have to be entertained again if the personality field is to realize its promise of understanding the total life style of persons. For these reasons and many more, to scrutinize the work and lives of Allport, Maslow, and Murray is to learn a great deal about the personality field.

We have had the help of many persons in preparing this book. We owe a special debt to Henry A. Murray who, as the lone survivor of our triumvirate, commented on our approach to his and the others' positions with great spirit, though not always perfect agreement. David Wexler also provided valuable information and comments. For proofreading, general reactions, and secretarial help, we are indebted to Rod Kessler, Judy Altman, and Audrey Derany. Finally, we wish to congratulate each other on the facility of our collaboration. Not only did we really help each other, but we grew in friendship all the while.

Contents

Introduction

These days in psychology one hears all sorts of talk—favorable and critical, open and clandestine, rational and emotional—about a gathering third force, a humanistic surging that will set the field straight, once and for all. Indeed, one of the theorists considered in this book, Abraham Maslow (1962), was responsible for the phrase, "the third force." The other two psychological forces, classical Freudianism and positivistic behaviorism, have dominated psychology for most of its recent history.

Nonhumanism and Humanism

Logical positivism and extreme behaviorism, with their emphases on observable responses rather than thoughts and feelings, external pressures rather than internal promptings, and only those concepts that can be clearly formulated no matter how trivial the result, can easily be considered nonhumanistic. Actually, under the influence of positivistic behaviorism, psychology became defined as "the science of behavior" rather than "the science of the mind, or psyche," and lower animals became more popular as subjects for study than humans. Under the sway of positivistic behaviorism, the human is hardly regarded as special, much less unique.

1

Why classical Freudianism may be regarded as nonhuman-istic is not as easily understood. After all, man is the only important subject for study in psychoanalysis, and thought and feelings certainly receive much more attention than mere observable responses. It is not, however, the topics or data of psychoanalysis that adherents to the third force find objec-tionable. Rather, third-force followers reject what they see as an attempt in Freudianism to manipulate and denigrate peo-ple, to deal with them in nonhuman ways. The problem with classical Freudianism is the nature of its explanations of hu-man behavior, not its subject matter *per se*.

Freudian explanations of human behavior emanate from certain assumptions[1] that betray a pessimistic attitude. For ex-ample, Freudianism assumes that man's inheritance is a set of selfish and animalistic instincts, and that a conflict between the individual and society is inevitable, since society is concerned with the common good. The only way to deal with such a conflict is to compromise by defending not only against direct expression but even against full awareness of the instinctual drives. Because society is the stronger of the two forces, the compromise must take the form of the individual subordinat-ing his instinctual gratification to social acceptability. As a functioning adult, the individual inhibits sexual and aggres-sive impulses, defends against embarrassing awareness of these impulses, and even suppresses memories of what he may have thought or done as a child. Since conflict between the individual and society is inevitable, it is assumed that un-conscious motivation and defensiveness are ubiquitous, and that man can never truly know himself. One implication of this is that pride in oneself and one's accomplishments, and trust in the veracity of one's experience and mentation, must always be to some degree a failure of humility. These as-sumptions about human behavior hardly convince third-force

1. See Maddi, 1968.

adherents that classical Freudianism conceives of man's thoughts, feelings, and actions as valuable *per se*. The aim of psychoanalysis seems to be to strip man of a sense of dignity, and convince him that he stands no higher than the other animals. For psychoanalysts to insist that they accept and love man, despite his weakness and follies, does not help much.

Humanism, as espoused by third-force adherents, leads to a psychology that is not only centered on the human being but sets a positive value on those of his capabilities and aspirations that seem to distinguish him from lower animals and make him the master of his own fate. Choice, will-power, conceptual thought, imagination, introspection, self-criticism, aspirations for the future, and creativity are important topics in humanism, for they refer to capabilities and interests that seem unique to man as a species. If these qualities are not, strictly speaking, unique to man, they are so highly developed in him that the humanistic position has a strong appeal for everyone, including psychologists.

Modern existentialism also contains an important message for third-force adherents, for only man is endowed with the ability to reflect on his own actions and question the meaning and value of his own existence. Suicide, as a negative conclusion to such questioning, seems to be an uniquely human phenomenon. Indeed, when one reviews the characteristics of man that seem so apparently to distinguish him from other species, it is difficult to understand why the humanistic position has so many opponents in contemporary psychology.

Humanism is not only concerned with the characteristics setting man apart from other living things. Also important are the characteristics that set each man apart from other men. Individuality—the thoughts, fantasies, strivings, worries, triumphs, and tragedies that sum up to one particular person's existence and no one else's—is always a central topic in humanistic positions. Indeed, it is common for humanistic psy-

chologists to assert that one cannot really understand behavior by studying separate parts of it in isolation. Complete
understanding requires putting all the parts together and employing a knowledge of the characteristics of wholes. The
same person who learns slowly in the classroom and is unable
to direct his attention effectively under scrutiny may well be
able to produce a masterpiece in the solitude of his own
home. To take any part of this person's behavior in isolation
from another—indeed, in isolation from many, many others,
such as the intensity and content of his interpersonal relationships or the nurturance and directedness of his parents' actions toward him—would be to fail in understanding what
was going on.

Many humanists assert that complete understanding is not
even merely a matter of putting all the parts of behavior together so that they make a whole. A whole is not necessarily
just the sum of its parts—it can and usually does have new
properties of its own. So, in our example, the person's in-
ability to function in groups having an evaluative connotation
may actually enhance, rather than detract from, his ability to
create in isolation. In order to appreciate this, one would
have to think of that person's creative functioning as an
unique and unpredictable outcome of the interaction of the
experiences and activities that comprise his life.

Finally, the focus on the experiences of the individual in
humanistic doctrines more or less requires that originality or
creativity will be an important topic for study. This requirement is virtually by definition, for the only way to be an individual is to be original. You must do the originating, for if
you merely borrow from someone else you will not have become an individual.

It should be apparent in all this that humanism takes a very
optimistic, laudatory view of man. In the history of philosophical thought, humanism has always made a hero of man,

and the contemporary third force in psychology is certainly no exception.

Humanism in Personology

If humanism were to have any thrust at all in psychology, it would certainly not be surprising to find the impact in personology, the field that concerns itself directly with man's most human characteristics, including what gives a person his unique manner and appearance, dictates his own particular influence on his world, and governs his own reactions to external pressures. When pursuing such concerns of personology, one almost inevitably compares the approaches to and solutions of life's problems by different persons, and in the process it is natural to ask such questions as how relatively adequate is a person's personality and how effective is his life style. Indeed, so natural are such questions that it is a rare theory of personality which does not contain some definition of mental health and illness, however worded, however explicit. The point to be recognized is that personology, by virtue of its subject matter, is heavily concerned with evaluations of man in his psychological endeavors. Humanism, as a stance, is a positive evaluation, an article of faith in man's capabilities that stands in contrast to those conceptualizations that are negative or neutral.

If it seems peculiar to assert that personology is by its nature an evaluative enterprise, some thought should be given to the evolution of psychology out of philosophy. In philosophy, the analogous field to personality is character, and the study of character would have little purpose if it did not concern ethics. The philosopher's distinction between virtue and vice is quite likely analogous to the psychologist's distinction between mental health and illness. With these points in mind, it does not seem surprising that so many personologists should have started out as clergymen, or the sons of clergymen. To be sure, there are important differences in the purposes and uses of evaluations made in personology and in philosophy, but all that is important here is to recognize that it is appropriate that humanism and other evaluative stances regarding man should find a place in personology.

Indeed, if personology is by its nature an evaluative enterprise, it would bespeak ineffectiveness not to make one's evaluations explicit. Asserting that one is not evaluating, that one is not being as arbitrary as philosophers, while one considers such topics as marital relations, intimate versus contractual relationships, the translation of fantasy into action, aggressiveness and competition as well as cooperation, work productiveness and efficiency, and so forth, is a dangerous kind of denial. The only way that personologists will get to do their inherently evaluative task well is to confront that task explicitly and discuss openly the merits and limitations of various evaluative positions. The three theorists to be considered in this book all agree with this proposition.

> I'm sorry that psychology has officially cut itself off from philosophy because this means no more than giving up good philosophies for bad ones. Every man living has a philosophy, an uncriticized, uncorrectable, unimprovable, unconscious one. If you want to improve it, and make it more realistic, more useful, and more fruitful, you have to be conscious of it, and *work* with it, criticize it, improve it. This most people (including most psychologists) don't do. (Maslow, 1956, p. 5)

Likewise, in an essay first published in 1954 dealing with "personalistic philosophy," Allport argued that the psychological analysis of human personality must come to terms with philosophy:

> Having made this pious disclaimer, let us hasten to admit that whether he knows it or not, every psychologist gravitates towards an ontological position. Like a satellite he slips into the orbit of positivism, naturalism, idealism, personalism. One of

these, or some other explicit philosophy exerts a pull upon his own silent presuppositions, even though he may remain ignorant of the affinity that exists. It is shortsighted of him to deny the dependence—or to refuse to articulate, as best he can, his own thinking about human nature with that brand of philosophy with which it is most closely allied. (Allport, 1960a, p. 17)

The Personologists Chosen for This Book

It would be surprising to find humanism only now entering personology, with its history of 70 years or more as a formal discipline. Nevertheless, some third-force adherents, carried away by their enthusiasm, invite one to believe that humanism in personology is new despite abundant evidence to the contrary. The choice of theorists for inclusion in this book was made with the value in mind of demonstrating this point. Gordon Allport, Abraham Maslow, and Henry Murray have been strong proponents of humanistic theories of personality over a continuous span of 30 to 40 years. Such long-standing articulate support of a position cannot be attributed merely to an opposition to Freud. Allport very early expressed such opposition, Maslow only more recently developed it, and Murray, a psychoanalyst, was heavily influenced by psychosocial conflict theory, though always cognizant of the limitations of Freud's point of view. Although Allport, Maslow, and Murray may have sometimes seemed like lonely voices in the wilderness of negative or neutral evaluations of man, they were voices nonetheless. It would be erroneous to dispute the current swelling of enthusiasm for humanism in personology, but it would be equally misleading to believe that contemporary psychology discovered the possibility of viewing man with optimism.

Allport, Maslow, and Murray were not chosen only because of their historical significance. These three theorists have had a deep and continuous influence on personology.

Murray's (1938) early research and theorizing on needs established the definitive format for personality research where comprehensive information was considered important. Personality tests still commonly utilize his list of needs as a starting point.[2] A survey has shown that, although Freud is the most influential theorist for clinical psychologists, Allport is ranked in second place[3]—an extraordinary finding, given Allport's strong opposition to the Freudian dynamic view. But it is Maslow, perhaps more than any other person, who is considered to be the formulator of contemporary humanism in psychology. Merely to list the psychologists who as students or colleagues have been directly influenced by one or another of these three theorists would be tantamount to a "Who's Who" in the field of personality theory and research.

The influence of Allport, Maslow, and Murray, moreover, has not been restricted to personology. Their views have also taken root in social psychology, psychotherapy, measurement, and religion. Perhaps the most comprehensive estimate of the impact of these three men is seen in both Allport's and Maslow's presidencies of the American Psychological Association and Murray's receipt of the Distinguished Scientific Contributions Award from that association. Leaving aside the attempt to understand humanistic emphases in personology, the personality theories of these three men are important enough in their own right to warrant more consideration than they receive here. Nevertheless, the fact that these personality theories are early expressions of humanism in personology adds to their interest. Through scrutinizing the nature of the assumptions of Allport, Maslow, and Murray and the data they find important, there is much to be learned about the strengths and weaknesses of a point of view that puts man in an optimistic light.

2. E.g., Edwards, 1963; Jackson, 1967; Stern, 1958b.
3. Cf., Hall and Lindzey, 1957.

The Organization of This Book

Although the works of Allport, Maslow, and Murray are widely known in psychology, familiarity alone does not make presenting and comparing their views a simple, straightforward task. The complications begin with the phenomena to be explained, for people are bewilderingly multifaceted and changeable in their manner of living. Moreover, these personologists have been uncompromising in their effort to encompass the entire personality, whatever the toll in conceptual complexity and indefiniteness. They have approached theory construction inductively, with sensitivity and imagination, concentrating more on completeness and an intuitive sense of accuracy than on formal elegance and precision. And if these did not make for complications enough, Allport, Maslow, and Murray, throughout long and productive careers, have felt free to follow their shifting apperceptions wherever they might lead, to a more compelling elaboration of a basic concept here, to the change of a general manner of thinking there.

For the sake of clarity in the face of such formidable difficulties, we have considered general orientations toward the nature of personality (what might be called metatheory) separately from the specific concepts and definitional statements that comprise the actual theories. There is so much material available that it has been necessary to select for presentation only what seems most central to the positions of each of these three men. In this, we have tried to avoid gross misinterpretations by using as a guide the theorists' recent writings and their explicit or implicit directives. Although differences as well as similarities are considered, care has been taken not to underscore small theoretical differences that may vanish as the language of the viewpoints of the three personologists becomes more specific.

The main purpose of the section on general orientations or

metatheory (Chapter one) is to show the large areas of con-
sensus among Allport, Maslow, and Murray, and to indicate
that the similarities are appropriately considered humanistic
stances. Although we have already suggested something of the
content of humanistic thinking in personology, the exploration of the metatheorizing done by Allport, Murray, and
Maslow will add considerable meat to our skeleton outline.
The plausibility of some point made by a theorist will sometimes be considered; however, a comprehensive evaluation
of humanistic metatheorizing about personality is not intended. After all, a metatheory is really no more than a set
of attitudes and opinions and, as such, is not really subject to
confirmation or disconfirmation by empirical findings.

Ample opportunity to observe how the humanistic metatheory influences the actual concepts and data selected for
consideration is provided in the sections on the formal theories
(Chapters two and three). In addition, information on the
similarities and differences in concepts, definitions, and data
is available. Since formal theories are supposed to be explanatory systems that contribute to the understanding of empirical
phenomena, rather than merely opinions and attitudes, it is
useful to evaluate the strengths and weaknesses of the theories.
The overall criterion of evaluation that will be employed is
that of usability. Focusing attention to usability of a theory
is not a novel undertaking. Consider the application of a
personality theory to the observed functioning of a particular
person or group. If the personality theory has been developed
to the point where it can be usefully applied to empirical
data, it first permits a decision as to whether the available
observations are within the range that the theory aims to
explain. If the observations are relevant, the theory provides
guide lines for their description according to a specified set
of data terms. Then it is possible to generate a precise explanation of the description by a deductive process that is
explicit and unambiguous. This explanation provides the basis

for deduction of equally precise predictions concerning events that have not yet been observed. In this entire process it is possible for competent and conscientious psychologists to reach substantial agreement, at each step, regardless of their preference or dislike for the theory.

Actually, the criterion of usability incorporates several of the criteria often employed in the evaluation of theory, and stems from certain assumptions concerning the nature of the enterprise of theorizing. A brief consideration of some of these assumptions will make the concept of usability more concrete by indicating some of the ways in which it is jeopardized.[4] In our view, a theory is a convention consisting of a number of interrelated concepts on different levels of generality. The most concrete concepts have the primary function of providing direct explanations of the observables or data. Data such as observed competitive actions toward others, an increase in anxiety level on entering a classroom, and a relatively high number of hours spent studying all might be explained by the construct "need for achievement." Similarly, a relatively large amount of time spent in the company of others, an interest in parties, and an increase of anxiety at the prospect of being alone are observables that could be explained by the concept "need for affiliation." In both cases, the explanation takes the form of pinpointing the functional equivalence of some observables that would not necessarily have been considered as similar otherwise. The relatively concrete concepts are the simplest levels of theory, and their applicability to the data at hand should be as straightforward as possible. For this reason, they should be unitary entities that cannot fruitfully be analysed into some set of simpler component parts. They are the "atoms" of a personality theory.

As they widen in terms of generality, concepts in a per-

---

4. For a more complete exposition, see Maddi, 1968.

sonality theory become complex structures, which subsume the more concrete concepts and establish the interrelationships among them. For example, one might adopt the concept of "Id" to refer to the inborn propensity for motivated activity, and subsume under it not only the needs for achievement and affiliation but many other needs as well. Specific statements concerning the nature of the relationship between this inborn tendency toward motivated activity and the various needs would also be made in a carefully developed theory. These relational statements might very well refer to the developmental or learning process whereby the inborn tendency is channeled into the need for achievement, or the need for affiliation, and not some other needs. In any event, it should be clear that the very general concepts in a theory do not refer directly to observables, but rather to more specific statements that in turn refer to observables. Whatever implications for data collection the general concepts have, they are subsidiary to the function of providing an integrative scheme that organizes and articulates a set of lower-order concepts.

Even from this most brief consideration of the nature of a personality theory, one can imagine some of the typical shortcomings that can limit its usability. It is difficult to use a theory if there is (1) imprecise or incomplete specification of the observables or data that are to be considered, (2) absence of relatively general concepts, relatively concrete concepts, or statements of relationship between the two, (3) vagueness due to the use of figurative, inconsistent or otherwise ambiguous language in the definition of concepts and the delineation of relationships, and (4) the adoption of concrete concepts that are inherently heterogeneous. With poor specifications of relevant observables, it becomes difficult to be sure that one is using the personality theory in the kinds of explanatory tasks for which it was intended. If relatively concrete concepts are omitted, then one must face the task of explaining observables with the very general concepts alone, a situation bound to produce unsatisfyingly vague results. If it is the relatively general concepts that are missing, the explanations based on concrete concepts will remain as odd, fragmentary bits of knowledge, contributing little to the "big picture." Without relational statements, one will not know how to put general and specific levels of knowledge together in any comprehensively satisfying way. It goes without saying that vagueness in any theoretical step will jeopardize usability, for a theory, like any other complex whole, is only as strong as its weakest link. Finally, the adoption of inherently heterogeneous concepts with which to explain observables directly will only lead to an inconsistent application of those concepts, especially when there are many of them in a theory.

Theories do not usually start out being usable. The cognitive operations underlying the creation of ideas are simply more indirect, idiosyncratic, and metaphorical than those that facilitate precise formulation and clarity in communication. The employment of usability as an evaluative criterion is premature when a theory is still in its early stages of development. But the theories of Allport, Maslow, and Murray had their beginnings more than 25 years ago, and hence consideration of their usability seems appropriate and even timely, insofar as it may provide suggestions relevant to their further development.

Developmental considerations, the relational statements made by Allport, Maslow, and Murray intended to link the relatively general concepts with the relatively concrete ones, are discussed in Chapter four. Given the unlearned, inherent aspects of man's nature with which we all begin life, what are the specific developmental experiences that determine the particular style of life each of us comes to have? Of special relevance in this chapter is the distinction between ideal and nonideal personalities, between mental health and illness. Developmental considerations loom large in understanding differentials in personal adequacy. As in Chapters two and three, in Chapter four the usability of the theorizing under scrutiny is discussed.

Through their formal theorizing, metatheorizing, and functioning as teachers, Allport, Maslow, and Murray have had a strong effect on personality research. This effect is traced in Chapter five. Each theorist has, of course, done research of his own. It is interesting to consider how this research expresses their metatheoretical and formal theoretical views, for herein lie insights into the nature of personality research emanating from humanism.

The meta and formal theories of Allport, Maslow, and Murray have also stimulated the research efforts of others. We will try to indicate some of these influences. What we write should not be construed as an appraisal of the empirical validity of the theories. The crucial evidence about empirical validity requires tests of predictions. Tests of predictions are premature—even unproductive, if attempted—until the theory is sufficiently well developed so that the kinds of facts that are actually relevant, and the precise manner in which the theory addresses itself to them, can be unequivocally discerned. Adequate development of a theory to the point where it is usable by the criteria mentioned before is a prior concern to that of testing empirical validity. Before adequate usability has been attained, empirical observations are probably best employed in theory construction. In general, it is more fruitful to consider the research relevant to the work of Allport, Maslow, and Murray as instrumental to the development and refinement of theory rather than to its definitive test.

Having considered the metatheories, formal theories, and research of these three personologists, what will remain to complete an investigation of their humanistic thrust is a consideration of their personal lives. This is the subject of Chapter six. We will be looking for whatever similarities can be found in the formative experiences of their lives. Hopefully, this analysis will tell us something of how they came to have those theoretical viewpoints they shared and those upon which they differed.

As you read the text, the following synopsis of the theories of Allport, Maslow, and Murray may be a useful guide.

Theoretical Summary of the Works of Allport, Maslow, and Murray

GENERAL CONSIDERATIONS

	MURRAY	ALLPORT	MASLOW
Definition or conception of personality	"A personality at any designed moment in its history . . . is the then-existing brain-lo-ated imperceptible and problematical hierar-chical constitution of an individual's entire stock of inter-related substance - dependent and structure depen-dent psychological properties."	"Personality is the dynamic organization within the individual of those psycho-physi-cal systems that deter-mine his characteris-tic behavior and thought."	"A personality syn-drome is . . . a structured, organized complex of apparently diversed specificities (behaviors, thoughts, impulses to action, perceptions, etc.) which . . . have a common unity that may be expressed variously as a similar dynamic meaning, ex-pression, "flavor," function, or purpose.
Proactive functioning	Man has internal processes and structures that have a causal influence upon perception, thought, feeling, and action.		
Role of exter-nal determi-nants	Allows sociocultural factors some promi-nence.	Tentative and quali-fied endorsement of external determinants in the case of highly structured situations.	Negligible influence.

	MURRAY	ALLPORT	MASLOW
Nature of interaction between proactive and external factors	Continual Conflict.	External factors usually function to set rather wide limits on the range of behavioral possibilities available to the person.	Closer to Allport for normals; closer to Murray for psychological.
Psychological organization	Regularity and order are typical; this is attributed to the unified organized nature of personality. There is both momentary (cross-sectional) and long-term (longitudinal) organization.		
Rationality	Presence and conflict of rational and irrational processes is seen in such things as odd inconsistencies, compulsions, and ego-alien acts.	Man's functioning is characteristically rational; governed by such conscious characteristics as long-range goals, plans of action and philosophies of life.	Presence and conflict of rational and irrational processes is seen in such things as odd inconsistencies, compulsions, and ego-alien acts.
Uniqueness	Some willingness to draw on cross-species comparisons. Allows for general concepts and laws. Nomothetic stance.	Man is unique as a species and individuals are unique. Extremely idiographic (morphogenic) position.	Needs are species wide but uniquely combined in people. Nomothetic stance.
Future orientation	Psychological growth, or progressively greater differentiation and integration, which seems to continue throughout life, is genuine, natural, and crucial to an understanding of man. Any approach that attempts to explain adult functioning as reflecting little more than sophisticated representations of early fixations, habits, and instincts misses the overwhelming importance of man's orientation towards future accomplishments and states of being.		

CONCRETE CONCEPTS
OF PERSONALITY

	MURRAY'S NEEDS	ALLPORT'S PERSONAL DISPOSITIONS	MASLOW'S NEEDS
Major effects	These concrete concepts (Need, Personal Dispositions) function to produce perceptions, interpretations, feelings, and actions that are equivalent in terms of meaning or purpose. Needs and dispositions must be understood as serving an organizing and integrating role in life, and cannot be defined in terms of some invariant and simple set of responses or environmental pressure.		

	MURRAY	ALLPORT	MASLOW
	Equivalences of meaning in the person's (1) inner state, (2) perception of external situation, (3) imagined goal, (4) direction of action, and (5) produced effect, if any.	Stimulus and response equivalences.	Emphasis on needs as organizing and creating action possibilities and external reality.
Uniqueness	More than one person can possess a particular need.	Unique to individual. The term "common traits" is a convenient fiction expressing that men possess a common human nature and culture.	Each need is present in every member of the human species, though expressions of needs may vary from person to person.
Situational determinism	Concept of press, or pressure from the environment, which can activate an already present need.	Low: Personal Dispositions considered to be motivational to some degree in that they cause behavior.	Low.
Susceptibility to arousal	Need-intensity is a function of level of gratification. The triggering action of some perceived situational pressure is necessary in order for the need to become an active determinant of functioning.	Little formal role given to the arousal of personal dispositions by particular features of the external situation. Dispositions are not aroused; rather, they exist continuously, having an ongoing effect upon functioning.	Needs are not triggered by external events—they do wax and wane depending upon levels of gratification.
Classificatory schemes	Activity needs: a) process needs. b) mode needs. Effect needs.	Cardinal dispositions. Central dispositions. Secondary dispositions.	Higher needs. Lower needs.
	Mental needs. Viscerogenic needs. Socio-relational needs. Creative needs. Negative needs.	Phenotypical dispositions. Genotypical dispositions.	Physiological needs. Safety needs. Needs for belongingness and love. Esteem needs. Need for self-actualization. Need for cognitive understanding.

	MURRAY	ALLPORT	MASLOW
Hierarchy of prepotency	Present.	Present.	Present.
Unconscious/ Conscious aspects	Needs can be conscious or unconscious.	Personal dispositions are, or can easily be made, conscious.	Needs can be conscious or unconscious.

GENERAL CONCEPTS
OF PERSONALITY

	MURRAY	ALLPORT	MASLOW
Establishments of personality	Id, Ego, Ego-ideal and Super ego.	Proprium.	Syndromes (types).
Concept of self	Ego, defined mainly in terms of mental, volitional capacities.	Proprium or phenomenal self.	Occasionally refers to self, but gives it little formal importance.

Development

The similarities among the three theorists' accounts of development include great emphasis upon an active, influential consciousness, the assumption (however vaguely formulated) of an inherent growth tendency, a view of development as continuing into adulthood with related emphasis upon the complex differentiations and integrations of maturity, and a belief that personality is largely learned.

Infant does at birth possess some personality in the form of acceptable and unacceptable id impulses. With more experience and socialization, he begins to develop an ego, then a super ego, then an ego ideal.	No inherited personality components common to all. Infant has little personality. His undifferentiated, opportunistic behavior is determined by on-going biochemical processes and environmental pressures.	Needs are considered "instinctoid," and therefore to some extent there is influence of heredity. Development through Stages of Need-Hierarchy toward self-actualization.
Five stages of early life: 1) Claustral 2) Oral 3) Anal 4) Urethral 5) Phallic	*Year 1:* First signs of consciousness take the form of recognizable experience of body (bodily sense).	

	MURRAY	ALLPORT	MASLOW
	Middle Age: Involves conservative recompositions of the already developed structures and functions.	*Years 2–3:* Beginnings of self identity and self-esteem.	
		Years 4–6: Some self-extension and self-image.	
	Senescense: Decrease of potentialities for new compositions and recompositions.	*Years 6–12:* Rational coping quality of proprium become apparent.	
		Adolescence: Propriate striving is in increasing evidence.	
		Adulthood: Involves vigorous expression of all the previously learned functions, culminating in such criteria of maturity as a philosophy of life.	
Position on learning	Murray assumes learning and appears to subscribe to general principles of reinforcement. Learned needs develop out of unlearned needs.	Learned dispositions are quite independent of the dispositions that may have lead to their formation: functional autonomy. Role of social forces is limited to providing necessary background conditions for adequate personality development.	Not clear whether Maslow subscribed to orthodox principles of reinforcement, such as contiguity of stimulus and response and tension reduction as basic of learning.

General Orientations Toward the Nature of Personality

Hall and Lindzey (1957, p. 4) observe that personality theorists have been rebels in their time, and to judge from the dissatisfaction of Allport, Murray, and Maslow with the orthodoxies of the last few decades, they are not exceptions to this generalization. Faithful rendition of the bases for the considerable impact these psychologists have had requires attention not only to their positively and consistently affirmed assumptions about the nature of man, but also to their enriching critical remarks, so often leveled against radical behaviorism and classical Freudianism.

Man is Proactive

Perhaps the most basic of the convictions shared by Allport, Maslow, and Murray is that man has internal processes and structures that have a causal influence upon perception, thought, feeling and action. Some of these internal characteristics, such as the instincts (Murray and Kluckhohn, 1956, pp. 23–24) and needs (Maslow, 1954, pp. 107–55) are endogenous; others, such as individual styles of life (Allport, 1961, pp. 266–67; Murray, 1959, pp. 32–33; Maslow, 1954, pp. 300–302), are learned. All three theorists feel that it is impossible to provide an adequate explanation of a person's functioning in any given situation solely by consideration of the external features of the stimulus situation. Hence, any approach that focuses exclusively, or even predominantly, upon external factors is a target for criticism. These approaches, "associationism of all types, including environmentalism, behaviorism, stimulus-response . . . psychology" (Allport, 1955, p. 8), have been pejoratively labeled "Lockean" by Allport, "Peripheralistic" by Murray (1938, pp. 5–11), and atomistic-reductionistic by Maslow (1954, p. 27). Among the assumed errors made by adherents to these views are a disregard of extensive observational, logical, and introspective evidence for proaction (Allport, 1961, pp. 24–28; Murray, 1959, p. 15; Maslow, 1954, pp. 22–26) and a treatment of personality as no more than a logically superfluous concept (Allport, 1961, p. 27). The three personologists could very well point to the extensive literature on individual and group differences in functioning under objectively similar stimulus conditions to bolster their position.

Although Allport, Maslow, and Murray have steadfastly given primary causal importance to internal characteristics, they have not overlooked the role of external factors. None of them sees much value in the behavioristic type of situational analysis, however, because it tends to oversimplify the subtlety and complexity of human interaction with the environment, and restricts the range of stimulus meaning considered. They feel more satisfied with cultural and sociological variables, such as peer group and role pressures.

Only Murray has given external determinants the most prominent place in his thinking. Recent elaborations of the positions of Allport, Maslow, and Murray still show this difference, although all three seem to be giving more weight than formerly to exogenous factors. Murray writes that under the long influence of such colleagues as Kluckhohn, he has " . . . come to think that no theoretical system constructed on the psychological level will be adequate until it has been embraced by and intermeshed with a cultural-sociological system" (Murray, 1959, p. 45). Murray has not abandoned primary emphasis on proactive, individual personality factors, nor has he embraced the extreme interactional position exemplified by Sullivan (Murray, 1959, pp. 30–31), but external determinants are given considerable importance. In contrast, Allport's (1961, pp. 165–95) endorsement of such determinants remained to the end tentative and qualified. He took pains to delimit the province of strong external instigation of functioning to those situations that are highly structured (ibid., pp. 178–79). And Maslow (1954, p. 75) was even less willing to accept situational determinism.

Allport, Maslow, and Murray also differ in their perceptions of the typical nature of the interaction between proactive and external forces. Murray (1959, pp. 45–56) emphasizes the almost continual conflict produced by the antagonism between the two sets of forces, while Allport (1961, p. 186) believed that external factors usually function to set rather wide limits on the range of behavioral possibilities available to the person, still leaving considerable latitude for proactive tendencies to be expressed without severe conflict. Although Maslow has been less explicit than the other two, he seemed more in agreement with Allport than Murray, except for psychopathological cases, where he moves closer to the latter theorist.

Man Possesses Psychological Organization

In man's proactive functioning, Allport, Maslow, and Murray find regularity and order to be typical, and attribute this to the unified, organized nature of personality. Allport (1961, pp. 376–91) found that the individual's behavior shows complex integration. Murray feels that "personality is a temporal whole and to understand a part of it one must have a sense, though vague, of the totality" (Murray, 1938, p. 4). He argues by analogy that the unending transaction of biochemical processes in the brain, the obvious bodily locus of personality, makes it unlikely that any but a holistic view is tenable. Maslow (1954, Chapter 3) was actually the strongest proponent of the three theorists for the holistic position, arguing that it is impossible to appreciate any one aspect of a person's behavior without reference to all other aspects as well. For Maslow, each aspect of personality actually fuses with, and therefore changes, each other aspect, making it unfruitful to do otherwise than speak in terms of complex wholes.

Allport, Maslow, and Murray recognize two aspects of psychological organization. The first is unity at a given moment, seen in the convergence of many personality characteristics in the determination of functioning (Allport, 1961, p. 377; Murray, 1938, p. 86; Maslow, 1954, p. 63). The second is unity over a longer period of time. In discussing this, these theorists maintain that at the beginning of life the infant responds as a whole (Allport, 1961, p. 377; Murray, 1938, pp. 38–39; Maslow, 1962, pp. 177–82). As he becomes older, the primitive unity gives way to a more sophisticated psychological integration of the various components of personality, differentiated from the earlier whole by learning (Allport, 1961, p. 377; Murray, 1938, pp. 38–39, 395–96). Integration is maintained through the development of more general, embracing characteristics as the process of differentiation leads to greater complexity (Allport, 1961, p. 377). Important in the organizational aspect of the psychological growth is the time-binding quality of cognitive processes (Murray, 1938, p. 49).

From the three theorists' view of psychological organization, associationistic positions and limited experimental approaches seem particularly inadequate.

I was slow to perceive that current psychological theories of behavior were almost wholly concerned with actions of relatively short duration, reflexes and consecutive instrumental acts which reach their terminus within one experimental session, rather than with long-range enterprises which take weeks, months, or years of effort to complete. . . . The behavior of animals can be explained largely by reference to attractive or repellent presentations in their immediate environment and/or to momentarily urgent and rather quickly reducible states of tension; whereas a great deal of man's behavior cannot be explained except by reference to persistent "self-stimulation" in accordance with a plan of action, which often involves the subject's commitment to a distal goal or set of goals, as well as to a more or less flexible (or rigid) temporal order (schedule) or subsidiary, or stage, goals. (Murray, 1959, p. 23)

Allport (1961, pp. 258–59) agreed with Murray, and expressed his opposition to most existing analytical approaches to personality.[1] He felt the approaches tended to slice personality in fictitious ways in an attempt to achieve simplification and understanding. Maslow (1966, 1968a) could not have agreed more, taking the position that the theorists recommend methods of study that involve as much as possible of the individual's functioning at one moment in time and over the course of time, and that they attempt to represent the interrelated nature of aspects of functioning, however difficult this may be.

For all their objection to narrow, particularistic approaches, both Murray and Allport recognize the importance of avoiding the seductive pitfall of holistic approaches, namely, that they encourage "those lazy white elephants of the mind—huge, catchall, global concepts signifying nothing" (Murray, 1959, p. 19). Murray hurls a challenge at exponents of this extreme that is fully as biting as that leveled at the opposite extremists:

The terms "personality-as-a-whole" and "personality system" have been very popular in recent years; but no writer, so far as I know, has explicitly defined the components of a "whole"

1. E.g., McClelland, 1951.

personality or of a "system of personality." When definitions of the units of a system are lacking, the term stands for no more than an article of faith, and is misleading to boot, in so far as it suggests a condition of affairs that may not actually exist. (Murray, 1959, p. 51)

Earlier, probably due to the demands of wartime conditions, Murray, who was working with the OSS staff, found it advisable or desirable to present a conception of the "personality as a whole" in contrast to a construct of the "whole personality." Starting with the acknowledgment that various people were using "whole personality" in reference to the total or entire personality, Murray distinguished two possible bases for the phrase: the whole longitudinal, or temporal, personality, and the whole cross-sectional personality.

Murray describes the whole longitudinal personality as being relatively concrete, referring to the entire sequence of organized psychological processes in the brain from birth to death. The cross-sectional personality, on the other hand, is very abstract and hypothetical: Personality is the entire constitution of potential psychological processes and structures in the brain at a given moment. Murray entertained the notion of combining these two definitions of the "whole" personality concept "into an all-inclusive notion which embraces not only the history of the proceedings of personality (longitudinal view), but the history of its developing establishment as portrayed by a series of cross-sectional formulations" (Murray, 1948, p. 45).

Considering a complete formulation of the development of the concept of the "whole personality" both impossible and undesirable, Murray proposed that several different formulations of the "personality as a whole" are sufficient for designated purposes, such as assessment or psychotherapy. Thus, it is not the whole, entire personality but the "personality as a whole"—"the over-all unity and organization of parts that is attained during a designated period of the subject's life. It refers to the degree of unity and coordination (wholeness)

that the personality exhibits during one short functional operation, or in a long series of progressions, day after day,
toward a distribution gradient, or in the establishment, over
a life-time, of a harmonious way of life which allows for the
successive satisfaction of its major needs" (Murray, 1948,
p. 46).

A similar note is struck by Allport (1955, pp. 36–41),
who considered it unwise to adopt an unelaborated, unde-
tailed form of the concept of self because doing so would
perpetuate the aura of mystery and the supernatural attending an unfathomable soul. Maslow was essentially mute on
this matter of holistic vagueness, and, as will be apparent later,
was actually less careful to avoid it in his formal theorizing
than were the other two.

As indicated by some of the previous quotations and other
statements, Allport (1961, p. 380) and Murray (1951a, pp.
19–21) have attempted to avoid holistic vagueness by focusing primarily upon the organizational characteristics of the
personality involving purposiveness. But little organization is
produced by the easily satisfied, and therefore relatively tran-
sitory, viscerogenic drives. Organization is primarily a function of those endogenous and learned purposes, such as life
goals (Allport, 1955, p. 49), dispositions to create (Murray,
1959, pp. 38–45), and competence motivation (White,
1959), that are nonspecific as to the particulars of goal states
and hence relatively insatiable and continuing. Secondary in
importance for unity are the less clearly purposive, more expressive styles of functioning (Allport, 1961, pp. 460–94).
Maslow (1954, pp. 179–86) certainly took the same route,
but was generally more content with unrefined versions of
his concepts than the other two theorists.

Man is Psychologically Complex

By emphasizing organization, Allport, Maslow, and Murray do not mean to imply that man's functioning is simple.

This functioning is staggeringly complex if one focuses upon the many different elements that develop through the process of differentiation. Indeed, in order to delineate the organization, it is necessary to observe the abstract or general features of functioning that can be grouped together into classes on the basis of equivalence of purpose or meaning. Considerable inference is involved in such observation.

Our three theorists are aware that the level of abstraction one chooses in analysing behavior will determine how complex that behavior appears. The important matter is to find the level of abstraction that does least violence to the vital qualities of human living. It is known for example that a quite concrete, relatively uninterpretive analysis stressing the physical characteristics of behavior would lead to a view of that behavior as very complex due to its great variability among and within individuals (Fiske, 1961). However useful such an approach is for some purposes, Allport, Murray, and Maslow would find it employing too low a level of abstraction to do justice to the psychological meaning of functioning.

Allport and Murray have also expressed dissatisfaction with the opposite extreme level of abstraction, exemplified by theories that rely rather exclusively upon concepts involving a very high level of abstraction and interpretation. Such theories typically make only a few discriminations, thus missing some of the important differences between aspects of functioning. This is the primary difficulty that led Allport to make the critical statement that Freud's "general picture of motivation makes personality almost a wholly reactive product of two archaic forces. . . . Of course we gladly grant that adult motives often reflect sex and aggression . . . yet we cannot believe that Freud does justice to the diversity, uniqueness, and contemporaneity of most adult motivation" (Allport, 1961, p. 208). Similarly, Murray finds that his chief objection to Freud's system "is the commonplace that . . . the

libido has digested all the needs contributing to self-preserva-
tion, self-regard, and self-advancement, together with a host
of others, and rebaptized them in the name of Sex" (Murray,
1959, pp. 37–38).

Allport and Murray favor the utilization of a moderate
level of observational abstraction, along with the higher level
that permits an understanding of organization, because they
are convinced that people have many different, changing, and
sometimes incompatible intentions, values, and styles that can
be expressed in different ways depending upon the environmental context. They believe that an adequate theory of
personality should permit an explanation of these complexities. This view makes Allport and Murray critical of oversimplified explanations (Allport, 1961, pp. 208–211; Murray,
1954, pp. 442–45; 1959, pp. 37–38, 43). Oversimplifica-
tion has occurred when the personality constructs used (1)
focus too exclusively upon the concrete physical characteristics of responses, predicting that a high level of consistency
will be found, (2) are so abstract and few in number that
psychologically useful distinctions are blurred, (3) are too
rudimentary, having been developed to account for animal
behavior, to yield adequate explanations at the human level
with its great range of behavioral potential and time-binding
features, and (4) are not employed within a system permitting an understanding of changes in patterns of functioning
over time.

Although Maslow agrees with the emphasis in the last
paragraph, he tended to work at a much more global, undifferentiated level of abstraction than the other two personologists. It is difficult to avoid the conclusion that Allport's and
Murray's criticisms of the Freudian penchant for overgenerali-
zation apply to Maslow as well. In his defense, Maslow might
have asked how one is ever to understand such holistic phenomena as love by references to single aspects of personality
(Maslow, 1962, 1967b).

Man's Functioning is Rational

With the exception of some recent developments within ego-psychology, Freudian theory has emphasized the view that man's behavior originates in, and is determined largely by, unconscious, inexorable, selfish, primitive impulses. It is true that Freud conceived of the ego as a realistic and therefore rational agent, but it was given a reactive role in determining functioning. According to this extreme view, whatever rationality man seems to express in thought processes involving planning, decision making and achieving intellectual understanding is in large measure a defensive use of cognition in order to conceal the underlying irrational impulses that are the basic determinants of functioning.

To Allport (1961, pp. 145–54), Freud's view of man seemed almost wholly wrong. Allport believed that the adult's functioning is characteristically rational, being governed by such conscious characteristics of personality as long-range goals, plans of action, and philosophies of life. The extreme Freudian position that Allport reacted against would not dispute that such phenomena exist, but these phenomena would not be considered independent, primary determinants of functioning. Allport's view of adult functioning would more likely be considered a justification after the fact of compelling action of the Id. In contrast, Allport believed that only children, who have yet to develop their personality fully, and the mentally ill, in whom the maturation of rational processes has been arrested or disrupted, come close to fitting the image of extreme Freudianism.

The positions of Murray (1938, pp. 46–47, 49–54) and Maslow (1954, pp. 205–28) on functioning, though less opposed to the classical Freudian view, are similar to that of Allport in that they invest man with a large measure of rationality. Rational and irrational processes are considered to exist together in the personalities of all men. The action of irrational unconscious processes is seen in such things as odd inconsistencies, compulsions, and ego-alien acts. But a large proportion of functioning proceeds according to the influence of plans, intentions, and values that are conscious and rational. To be sure, some men are more rational than others, and the least rational are among those likely to be considered mentally ill, but Murray and Maslow do not make the sharp distinction between health and illness, adulthood and childhood, that is found in Allport.

It is largely the rationality they attribute to man that leads Allport, Maslow, and Murray to take subjective experience and self-report to be data of cardinal importance for an understanding of functioning (Allport, 1953, pp. 108–110; Murray, 1959, pp. 9–11; Maslow, 1968a, pp. 8–12). If people are rational, they will know themselves, and be able to give adequate accounts and predictions of their own behavior. One result of Allport's more extreme view of functioning is that he believed projective techniques to be quite useless for normal adults. One can obtain, he asserts, the same information by the much more simple method of asking the person, provided he has resolved to be frank. Murray (1938, pp. 114, 530–31) and Maslow (1954, pp. 22–24, 101) are more convinced that projective techniques are important, as these techniques tap the areas of unconsciousness and irrationality that exist in all of us. But the data of projection are not sufficient, requiring supplementation by direct self-report.

Allport's position is so extreme that it seems unlikely to be strongly supported by empirical findings. Take as an example research on achievement need and achievement value (McClelland, 1958, p. 37). The need score is based on the content analysis of TAT stories, while the value score involves the individual's answers to a set of questions about achievement. There is only a very low positive correlation between the projective measure and the more direct measure of value or attitude (deCharms, Morrison, Reitman, and McClelland,

1955), indicating that the two tap largely different aspects of functioning. As the need score is not related to direct self-ratings of achievement drive, it seems likely that it reflects at least partly unconscious strivings. If Allport's position was tenable, then the need score would be superfluous in understanding the functioning of normal people. For that matter, if Freud's position was adequate, then the achievement value score would not be particularly useful. But each of these scores is related to other, different aspects of functioning (McClelland, 1958, pp. 38–40). The need score correlates with aspects of memory and performance, and the value score, though not related to these, correlates with suggestibility in an ambiguous situation. Each of the scores seems to be tapping a different, though meaningful, aspect of personality. As the scores may reflect different degrees of consciousness, the positions of Murray and Maslow seem supported more than do those of Allport or Freud. Arguments of the type presented here are of limited relevance, however, not only because the empirical facts are incomplete at this stage of research but also because the variables involved would often be considered artificial representations of personality by Allport.

Man is Psychologically Unique

Allport was more extreme on the question of uniqueness than were Maslow and Murray. For Allport (1955, p. 22), man is so unique as a species that an approach to understanding his functioning that utilizes lower animals is virtually useless. Although Murray has criticized the "audacious assumption of species equivalence" (Murray, 1954, p. 435) made by learning theorists, he is less extreme concerning the uniqueness of man, as shown by his willingness to draw certain conclusions about the human species on the basis of cross-species comparisons (Murray, 1959, pp. 14–19). With similar emphasis, Maslow (1964, pp. 1–15) theorized about a specific set of needs that characterize every member of the human species, though he did believe that these needs could find different expressions in different persons.

The disparity in emphasis on uniqueness between Allport on the one hand and Maslow and Murray on the other is still apparent when the focus shifts to the difference between individual members of the human species. To Allport, "each person is an idiom unto himself, an apparent violation of the syntax of the species" (Allport, 1955, p. 19). In explicating this position, Allport focused upon the apparently limitless range of potential behavior available to man by virtue of a big brain and a relative absence of instincts (ibid., p. 22), and ventures the opinion "that all of the animals of the world are psychologically less distinct from one another than one man is from other men" (ibid., p. 23). All this is strong medicine that could kill the patient—psychology—already in a fever over the struggle for general laws that psychologists believe would make its scientific status indisputable. To anyone engaged in this struggle, Allport's position must seem cruel heresy, and hence, further consideration of it is in order.

Allport (1937, p. 4) argued that the major task of psychology is to understand and predict the individual case, rather than the contrived average case. Now if nomothetic concepts and laws, derived from and applicable to the data of aggregates, were completely adequate for predicting each individual case, there would seem to be little purpose in Allport's championing of the inviolacy of individuality. In practice, however, perfect prediction and understanding using general laws is never achieved. Indeed, there is often a sizable minority of cases to which the general law does not seem to apply. This is not surprising to Allport (1961, pp. 332–56), who believed that nomothetical concepts were merely convenient fictions useful only insofar as they may resemble the true personality of some people. If a moderate degree of understanding and predictive accuracy were sufficient to satisfy the investigator, Allport would not have been seriously opposed to the nomothetic approach. But the paramount goal of psychology requires a greater approximation to the truth.

In an attempt to achieve the paramount goal of psychology, it will be necessary, according to Allport, to develop laws that are derived from and applicable to the data of each individual case alone. At first he called such laws idiographic (Allport, 1937, pp. 3–23), and seemed to conceptualize the laws in such an extreme fashion that virtually no generalization across persons would be possible (1942, p. 57). A concept developed to explain some behavior of one man would, strictly speaking, not be applicable to anyone else. More recently Allport (1961, pp. 357–61; 1962) substituted the term morphogenic for idiographic, and seems to be formulating a position that is less extreme, permitting the use of concepts that are in principle not restricted in applicability to only one person. Allport's emphasis is still overwhelmingly on concepts and laws that reflect the individuality of the person studied, but it is at least considered possible that those concepts and laws would turn out to apply to some other people as well. Allport makes a strong plea for freedom from the restricting nomothetic mold of the other sciences, which he believes have not been confronted with uniqueness on a grand scale, and has more recently offered a number of suggestions for concrete morphogenic methods of study (Allport, 1962).

Allport's view of man's psychological uniqueness poses an alternative to the traditional view of science that he believed would lead to the highest level of prediction and control. Although the morphogenic approach should certainly be tried in research, it raises a keen sense of futility when couched as a replacement for an approach encouraging generalization across persons. Must knowledge of individuals remain as unrelated, odd bits of information? How can significant systematization of knowledge be achieved? It should be established with certainty that nomothetic methods have been adequately tested before they are discarded on the grounds that they typically leave many individual cases unexplained.

Whether or not other sciences have been faced with overwhelming uniqueness, they certainly do recognize the necessity for deduction, from the general law and the characteristics of the situation involved, of explanations and predictions that apply to the specific case. For such deduction to be done well, the general law must provide exhaustive specifications of the conditions under which it does and does not apply, and the investigator must have sufficient knowledge of the concrete prediction situation in order to determine whether or not he should use the law. Furthermore, complex phenomena may well call for the application of more than one law, and, hence, the relationships between laws must be clearly specified. Only if all this information is available will it be possible to evaluate the explanatory adequacy of nomothetic methods, and even then particular general laws may turn out to be incorrectly formulated without this constituting a demonstration of the inadequacy of the methods they represent. The degree of theoretical and methodological care and precision involved in the adequate application of nomothetical methods is not often recognized as important or attempted in psychology, and hence, as McClelland (1951, pp. 89–94) suggests, the development of really useful general laws may be stifled, and individuality may loom overly large as an explanatory problem.

In practice, Murray's (1954, pp. 441–42; 1956, p. 10) position on the uniqueness of each member of the human species is more moderate. Although he recognizes important differences between people, he also considers areas of substantial similarity. General concepts and laws are quite useful in that they provide adequate understanding of those features of personality which are similar in most men. For complete understanding of each individual, however, additional information of a more specific variety is needed. Like Allport, Murray (1938) has emphasized the clinical method of observational study in all its detail. He has also utilized many different testing situations and instruments for each individual. In this detailed, rich approach to the study of human beings, Murray seems to be groping not only for general laws, but also for the knowledge necessary to apply them meaningfully to the individual case.

Maslow's (1954, 1955) position on the uniqueness of man is much like Murray's. Projective techniques, observation, direct self-report, and performance tests are all appropriate sources of information for Maslow, and are used in reaching generalizations applicable to all people, and to subgroups or types of people in particular. This is a nomothetic stance, in Allport's terms, even though Maslow, even more than Murray, argued for the importance of understanding each person's own special quality. But in this search for individuality, Maslow did not insist that a concept appropriate for one person is by definition irrelevant to someone else.

Man is Future Oriented

According to Allport, Maslow, and Murray, any approach that attempts to explain adult functioning as reflecting little more than sophisticated representations of early fixations, habits, and instincts misses the overwhelming importance of man's orientation toward future accomplishments and states of being. The three personologists take the psychological growth, or progressively greater differentiation and integration, that seems to continue throughout life to be genuine, natural, and crucial to an understanding of man. Important to this position is a view of personality as an open system that is continually transacting with environmental contexts (Allport, 1960a; Murray, 1959, p. 16; Maslow, 1954, pp. 74–75).

To Allport, such phenomena as evolving philosophies of

life, long-range goals, and a sense of personal integrity are not to be confused with the childhood tendencies toward response-repetition instilled by authoritative figures through manipulation of extrinsic rewards and punishments, or with the outcomes of early psychosexual conflicts. In a work with the revealing title of *Becoming,* Allport (1955) chided behavioristic and Freudian psychologists for not taking personally valued and intended development seriously: He concluded that Freudians are busy tracing the individual back into the past, while he is continually straining toward the future (Allport, 1953, pp. 108–110). Allport's (1955, pp. 28–33) position is so extreme that he found normal development after the first year or so to be significantly different from the earlier beginnings.

Murray (1938, pp. 282–396) has given more weight to enduring early learning, making his position, once again, more moderate than that of his colleague Allport. In fact, one of Murray's (ibid., pp. 360–85) contributions is an elaboration of the psychosexual stages of development and the complexes deriving from each of them. But Allport's criticism is echoed in Murray's belief that Freud's theory was incomplete, even though it had the virtue of beginning at the beginning, because it "never reached the consummation of the allegory, the heroic adult and his tragic end" (Murray, 1959, p. 13).

Like Murray, Maslow (1962, pp. 42–56) gives more weight to the formative effects of early learning. But the major thrust of Maslow's (1967, 1968a) position is to understand man's gropings toward an individuality that expresses his own particular potentialities. As man ages, and grows in experience, he becomes less predictable than he was in his early beginnings, less a creature of habit, and more a vigorous human being in the process of creating himself. Only when a person has been maimed by a destructive early environment is his life other than future oriented and changing.

In explaining present behavior on the basis of the rigidify-

ing effects of early experience, behavioristic and extreme
Freudian approaches have both assumed that the major principle governing man's functioning is the homeostatic tendency
to return to, or maintain, a rather steady, low level of organismic tension. People tend to repeat behavior that has been
followed by tension reduction as long as this association continues to some minimal degree. This is an argument on
adaptational grounds favoring the persistence of early learn-
ings because they were, and remain, successful in reducing
tension.

Allport, Murray, and Maslow agree that this conceptualization of man's functioning is not adequate as a basis for
explaining future-oriented, complexly organized behavior,
which seems to precipitate, rather than reduce, high levels of
tension, and is not primarily a repetition of past responses.
To support this criticism, these theorists could have recourse
to the rapidly accumulating research evidence that lower
organisms and man often engage in such seemingly arousing
activities as the exploration of new or changed portions of
stimulating surroundings and the avoidance of monotonous
surroundings through various forms of response variation
(Fiske and Maddi, 1961). In his criticism, Allport pointed
out that even Cannon, who invented the concept of homeostasis, could not have meant it to be used as the only principle
governing functioning and yet have said "with essential needs
answered through homeostasis, the priceless unessentials
could be freely sought" (Allport, 1961, p. 250). To Allport
(1955, pp. 63–68), there must be another principle that ap-
plies to the many aspects of functioning that are not simply
attempts to survive. Maslow (1955) was completely in agreement with this view, emphasizing that man, in his most human
activities, actually tolerates and even enjoys increases rather
than decreases in tension. Although agreeing that the simple
conception of homeostasis adopted by many psychologists is
inadequate, Murray favors an elaboration and extension of that

conception rather than the addition of a new one (Murray and Kluckhohn, 1956, pp. 36–37).

General Orientation Toward Theorizing

Allport, Maslow, and Murray are all displeased by certain disparaging attitudes toward theorizing that hold considerable sway in psychology. They see these attitudes as stemming in part from the influence of the doctrines of logical positivism and operationism.

The first of these unfortunate attitude's toward theorizing is a distrust of the method as a sound, useful means of gaining understanding. One reflection of this distrust is a belief that theory tends to divert one from the pursuit of truth.[2] The most direct and veridical way to build a science is through the continuing accumulation of empirical facts—these facts to be arrived at through simple methodological manipulations and extensions. Exponents of this view entertain the hope that facts will automatically fall into place at some future time when there are enough of them, thus providing us with the neat empirical generalizations that will make all behavior perfectly understandable. Another form of distrust of theorizing is the claim that theoretical constructs are logically superfluous, usually because they seem to be unnecessary, descriptive terms inserted between the stimulus and response variables of single experiments.[3]

The perverse opaqueness of uninterpreted facts is one reason for believing that theory is a diversion from the pursuit of truth. Uninterpreted facts show little inclination to fall into place and yield an inherent measure of understanding. They must be made understandable and orderly by the interpretations of the scientist, who can then use his interpretations as a powerful tool for creating new facts that may or may

2. E.g., Skinner, 1950.
3. E.g., Bolles, 1958.

not justify his theorizing. The view that theoretical constructs are superfluous overlooks the fact that a basic advantage of such constructs is their generality. This generality permits the results of many experiments to be joined together, and to suggest new experiments. It is shortsighted to argue that such concepts are unnecessary because particular experiments can be made intelligible without them.

The neglect of the synthetic, imaginative processes of thought represented in these two anti-theoretical views is anathema to Allport, Murray, and Maslow. A major procedural disadvantage of these anti-theoretical views is a proliferation of isolated experiments and lines of evidence. Without 'active theorizing, there can be little comprehensive unification of facts toward the goal of understanding the way a man lives his life. Embracing an anti-theoretical position seems not only wasteful of the investigator's capabilities, but may even constitute an advocacy of the impossible, and in that sense be dangerously misleading. When an avowedly anti-theoretical scientist discovers a fact, that fact owes its existence in large measure to the intuitive, preformal theorizing that preceded his research. Some scientists of this conviction might even admit that their hunches play a role in their choice of methodological manipulations but, instead of considering these intuitions as valuable foundations for theory, they are disregarded, presumably because they are either considered private, and therefore beyond the realm of science, or else quite incidental to the discovered fact. If some level of theorizing is an unavoidable part of the process of generating data, however, then overlooking this increases the risk of missing the vital facts of functioning, because the implicitly held theoretical frame of reference is not considered carefully as to its logical adequacy and reasonableness.

It happens that one of my inductions from experience is that many of those who spend most time asserting their immaculate empiricism are somewhat below average in their awareness of the distorting operation of their own preferences and ambitions and, therefore, are more liable than others to sally forth with reductively incongruent versions of reality. (Murray, 1959, p. 29)

The doctrines of logical positivism and operationism are best considered tools for theorizing rather than substitutes for theory. Indeed, their instrumental use in psychology has produced a valuable rise in standards of objectivity and precision in finding facts and formulating theory. Yet this usage, carried to an extreme, embodies the second attitude prevalent in psychology that Allport, Murray, and Maslow find objectionable. For them, to require a great deal of rigor in thought and experiment at this preliminary stage of our understanding of personality will be to stunt the vigorous, rich development of the field.

One specific effect of a premature emphasis on rigor is a focus upon those aspects of man's functioning that can be most easily formulated in precise, operational fashion. Such a focus invariably means the exclusion of subjective, internal, less readily observable states from consideration either as data or concepts. Another specific effect of premature concern with rigor is to favor the simplest, most readily conceived models for the explanation of man's functioning.

To Allport, Maslow, and Murray, excluding subjective states from study is to do such violence to the rich, multi-faceted, mainly internal processes of living as to obviate comprehensive understanding. Although it is admittedly difficult to study subjective states adequately, it is by no means impossible; it is not only potentially rewarding but indispensable. The personologists advocate personal introspection as a basis for study and conceptualization of the subjective states of others. Allport (1955, p. 23) says that it is in considering ourselves that we are led to an appreciation of uniqueness; Maslow (1954, p. 203) clearly theorized largely by observing himself and his friends; and Murray argues that "the need to describe and explain varieties of inner experience decided the original, and, I predict, will establish the final orientation of psychology" (Murray, 1938, p. 47). In what seems a mildly exasperated plea for clear recognition that the scientific study of so-called subjective phenomena is possible, Murray quotes effectively from Bridgman concerning the operational treatment of emotional states (Murray, 1938, p. 126).[4]

Equally dangerous to comprehensive understanding is the tendency of premature emphasis upon scientific rigor to lead to the adoption of very simple theoretical models. This and the additional danger that the ambiguous, complex subject matter of man's functioning will provoke tenacious faith in the simple models are aptly pinpointed in Allport's statement that "narrow systems, dogmatically held, tend to trivialize the mentality of the investigator and his students" (Allport, 1955, p. 17). Murray agrees when he says of premature emphasis upon rigor that "it is liable to seduce some promising psychologists away from the study of personalities—the domain that is theirs, and only theirs, to explore, survey, and map— away from the humanistically important riddles which we should be creeping up on gradually and craftily" (Murray, 1959, p. 8). In making the same point, Maslow said:

Most graduate training . . . turns away from [topics like love, hate, hope, fear]. They are called fuzzy, unscientific, tender-minded, mystical. What is offered instead? Dry bones. Techniques. Precision. Huge mountains of itty-bitty facts, having little to do with the interests that brought the student into psychology. Even worse, they try most often successfully, to make the student *ashamed* of his interests as if they were somehow unscientific. And so often the spark is lost, the fine impulses of youth are lost and they settle down to being members of the guild, with all its prejudices, its orthodoxies. (Maslow, 1957, p. 229)

4. E.g., Murray, 1938.

It is not even the existence of oversimplified approaches that was most objectionable to Allport, but, rather the tenacious, dogmatic propagandizing of them. Allport called for an air of intellectual ferment when he said that "censure should be reserved for those who would close all doors but one. The surest way to lose truth is to pretend that one already wholly possesses it" (Allport, 1955, p. 17). Murray (1951a, p. 436) advocates to anyone attempting to understand a phenomenon as complex and enigmatic as personality that he take seriously and immerse himself in the painful, tedious, difficult processes of collection and classification of a great variety of human behavior before making many theoretical pronouncements. According to Maslow (1968b), psychologists should resist the temptation to adopt oversimple solutions in the face of cognitive and professional pressure toward certainty before more adequate comprehensive solutions become possible. To this end, Allport (1961, p. 457) and Murray (1954, p. 436) suggest careful consideration of the point of view of an old authority, Aristotle, who said "it is the part of an educated man to seek exactness in each class of subjects only so far as the nature of the subject admits." And personality is at present a horrendously complicated subject.

Psychology Should be Socially Relevant

Our three theorists agree that the full and adequate understanding of man's functioning is a serious matter of the utmost importance, and hence is worth the undivided attention of psychologists. In discussing some of the reasons for his shift from physiology to psychology, Murray says that "influential in some degree (was) the impression . . . that human personality, because of its present sorry state, had become *the* problem of our time—a hive of conflicts, lonely, half-hollow, half-faithless, half-lost, half-neurotic, half-delinquent, not equal to the problems that confronted it, not very far from proving itself an evolutionary failure" (Murray, 1959, p. 11). Maslow agreed.

> If we die in another war or if we continue being tense and neurotic and anxious in an extended cold war, then this is due to the fact that we don't understand ourselves and we don't understand each other. Improve human nature and you improve all. . . . We need psychology. . . . The psychologist has a call then, in the same sense that a minister should have. He doesn't have the right to play games and to indulge himself. He has special responsibilities to the human race. . . . He ought to have a sense of mission, of dedication. (Maslow, 1957, p. 227)

But psychologists are failing to recognize and meet their share of responsibility to contribute to man the scientific rather than mystical knowledge of himself that would help him to lead a more effective life, and indeed, to preserve himself.

> Up to now the "behavior sciences," including psychology, have not provided us with a picture of man capable of creating or living in a democracy. . . . They have delivered into our hands a psychology of an "empty organism," pushed by drives and molded by environmental circumstance. . . . But the theory of democracy requires also that man possess a measure of rationality, a portion of freedom, a generic conscience, propriate ideals, and unique value. We cannot defend the ballot box or liberal education, nor advocate free discussion and democratic institutions, unless man has the potential capacity to profit therefrom. In *The Measure of Man,* Joseph Wood Krutch points out how logically the ideals of totalitarian dictatorships follow from the premises of "today's thinking" in mental and social science. He fears that democracy is being silently sabotaged by the very scientists who have benefited most from its faith in freedom of inquiry. (Allport, 1955, p. 100)

Murray (1962) strikes an only somewhat less condemnatory note in his vision of the future, in which psychology is found wanting for not having contributed to man the knowledge of himself that would have circumvented nuclear holocaust, but then is recognized as having been too much in its adolescence, too much concerned with scientific respectability and the readily studied fringe details of human behavior, to be held accountable for neglecting its responsibility to mankind.

Concluding Remarks

There are some basic agreements between Allport, Maslow, and Murray in their beliefs concerning the nature of personality. To all of them, man's functioning shows (1) the determining influence of internal, self-initiating characteristics more than of external forces, (2) both momentary and long-term organization, (3) complexity in the sense of change and the possession of many distinguishable elements, (4) the rationality of conscious intent, choice, and planning in greater magnitude than the irrationality of unconscious, irresistible impulses, (5) a large degree of species and individual uniqueness, and (6) the future orientation of continuing purpose and a tendency toward psychological growth. Murray takes a more moderate position on some of these points than does Allport. Leaving the differences in emphasis aside, however, it is clear that the overall views of the three theorists are humanistic ones that accord man a measure of dignity and excellence consistent with his high evolutionary status and accomplishments.

The humanistic orientations of Allport, Maslow, and Murray are often eloquently expressed.

It is generally assumed by the uninformed and innocent that all psychologists must have at least one "orienting attitude" in common: a stout affection for human beings coupled with a consuming interest in their emotions and evaluations, their imaginations and beliefs, their purposes and plans, their endeavors, failures, and achievements. But this assumption, it appears, is not correct. A psychologist who has been constantly prodded and goaded by these propulsions, as I have been, belongs to a once small and feeble, though now expanding and more capable minority. (Murray, 1959, p. 9)

Some theories of becoming are based largely upon the behavior of sick and anxious people or upon the antics of captive and desperate rats. Fewer theories have derived from the study of healthy human beings, those who strive not so much to preserve life as to make it worth living. Thus we find today many studies of criminals, few of law-abiders; many of fear, few of courage; more on hostility than on affiliation; much in the blindness of man, little on his vision; much on his past, little on his outreaching into the future. (Allport, 1955, p. 18)

One major shortcoming of research psychology (and of psychiatry as well), is its pessimistic, negative and limited conception of the full height to which the human being can attain. Partly because of this preconception, it has so far revealed to us much about man's shortcomings, his illnesses, his sins and his weaknesses, but rather little about his virtues, his potentialities, or his highest aspirations. . . . This is not a call for optimism. Rather it is a demand for realism in the best and fullest sense of that word. To identify realism with darkness, misery, pathology and breakdown as so many novelists have done in our time, is idiotic. Happiness is just as real as unhappiness, gratification is just as real as frustration, love is just as real as hostility. . . . We must know what men are like at their best; not only what they *are,* but also what they can become. . . . My own belief is that such a health-psychology will inevitably transform our deepest conceptions of human nature. (Maslow, 1957, p. 236)

These words, though expressing bitterness and dissatisfaction toward some psychologists, have none of the pessimism and cynicism toward man in general seen in such approaches as classical Freudianism, which generalizes from psychopathology to all of man's functioning, and extreme behaviorism, which finds equivalences between the rat and the human. It is of considerable importance that Allport, Murray, and Maslow developed their heroic views of man from considering normal and exceptional people.

Returning to the statement made by Hall and Lindzey (1957) with which this section was begun, it seems that Allport, Murray, and Maslow have been rebels in one sense only. They have promulgated a view of man that was at first, and to some extent still is, outside the main stream of psychological orthodoxy in this country. The particulars of their view, however, are very old, and are held at this time by many people—intellectuals and thoughtful men, artists and scientists—outside of psychology proper.

Because they are created by personalities, theories of personality will show the influence of the beliefs, values and motives of their creators. As an introduction or background to the formal theories of Allport, Maslow, and Murray, this presentation has provided ample evidence of a humanistic view and of tolerance for ambiguity with a concomitant interest in that which is not easily formulated.

2

The Formal Theories: Relatively Concrete Concepts

Definition of Personality

Although Allport, Maslow, and Murray define personality in different words, all three theorists include quite similar characteristics in their definitions. Allport has modified his definition of personality very little over the years. To him, "personality is the dynamic organization within the individual of those psychophysical systems that determine his characteristic behavior and thought" (Allport, 1961, p. 28). It is more difficult to point to any single definition of personality expressed by Murray, although he has considered personality to be the hypothetical structure of the mind, the consistent establishments and processes of which are manifested over and over again (together with some unique or novel elements) in the internal and external proceedings that constitute a person's life (Murray and Kluckhohn, 1956, p. 30). Thus, personality is not a series of biographical facts but something more general and enduring that is inferred from the facts. More recently, Murray has developed a more complicated, though generally similar definition:

A personality at any designated moment in its history . . . is the then-existing brain-located, imperceptible and problematical

hierarchical constitution of an individual's entire stock of interrelated substance-dependent and structure-dependent psychological properties (elementary, associational, and organizational). (Murray, 1968, p. 6)

It is even more difficult to find one authoritative definition
of personality in Maslow's writings, but there is one which can
be considered at least representative of his approach:

Our preliminary definition of a personality syndrome is that it
is a structured, organized complex of apparently diverse specificities (behaviors, thoughts, impulses to action, perceptions,
etc.) which . . . have a common unity that may be expressed
variously as a similar dynamic meaning, expression, "flavor,"
function, or purpose. (Maslow, 1954, p. 32)

With varying degrees of explicitness, all these definitions
of personality distinguish between the internal characteristics
that form the personality (whether they be called "psychophysical systems," "establishments," or "dynamic meanings"),
and the aspects of functioning, or behavior or data that are
determined by the characteristics. Murray's second definition
may seem to deviate from this formula, but the rest of the
section from which it has been drawn indicates clearly that
"properties" are underlying characteristics of personality that
are expressed in various ways in the person's behavior. Also
common to the definitions of personality is an emphasis on
personality as an organizer, an integrator of experience. Less
explicit, but also present, is the implication that personality
defines the uniqueness, or specialness, of the person's life.

Data Language

Theories always make some specification of the observables, or data, to which they are properly applied. Especially
because complex phenomena such as man's functioning can
be described in many different ways, it is important to com-

pare the data language, or protocol statements (Mandler and Kessen, 1959), that the theories of Allport and Maslow employ.

Allport's definition of personality indicates that the facts he wishes to explain are the characteristic thoughts and behaviors of the individual. The terms *behavior* and *thought* "are a blanket to designate anything whatsoever an individual may do" (Allport, 1961, p. 29). The term *characteristic* is merely a redundancy to emphasize individuality. Allport's theory specifies virtually no data language beyond this. It is not very conducive to the consistent usage of a theory to say that it pertains to everything the individual may do, without detailing the types of things that are to be recognized.

Maslow was perhaps a bit more specific. The data term in his definition of personality (that is, specificities) is meant to include such things as behaviors, thoughts, impulses to action, and perceptions. These are presumably the kinds of variables that he wished to explain through his personality theory. To be sure, Maslow's emphasis on behaviors and thoughts has the same blanket quality found in Allport's data specification, with whatever greater specificity available to Maslow being carried in the terms "impulses to action" and "perceptions." But these terms are also very general, and are subject to many diverse interpretations in popular usage. Maslow did not improve matters by indicating that the list of data terms offered is not exhaustive, but only exemplary. It must be concluded that he went little beyond Allport in providing a consistent data language that is adapted to his theorizing.

Murray, more than his fellow theorists, has attempted serious specification of the data units to which his theory is to apply. These units, as can be seen from his definition of personality, are called *proceedings*. A proceeding can very roughly be identified by the initiation and completion of "a dynamically significant pattern of behavior" (Murray, 1951a,

p. 269) that involves real or imagined interaction between
the subject and an animate or inanimate aspect of his environment. Real or *external proceedings* might include a conversation concerning the Berlin crisis or the construction of a sail-
boat model, while imagined or *internal proceedings* might
include the solitary attempt to solve a mathematics problem
or daydreaming of a seduction. The most important proceedings are those involving interpersonal behavior. It is typical
for a number of proceedings to overlap during any particular
unit of time, or *period*. Murray also feels it necessary to recognize the meaningful sequence of proceedings, by which,
"a directionally organized intermittent succession of proceedings, may be called a *serial*. Thus, a serial (such as a friendship, a marriage, a career in business) is a relatively long
functional unit which can be formulated only roughly" (Murray, 1951, p. 272).

Allport and, to some extent, Maslow, are apparently content to consider any of the many possible data terms that
can be conjured up by anyone. Murray is more selective, attempting to focus upon terms that seem to him more vital
to living than those, for example, that would be based exclusively on the concrete physical characteristics of actual
movements. Although one gets a general sense of the temporal, purposive quality of behavior that he finds important,
it must be said that the definitional statements associated
with such terms as *proceeding* and *serial* are not sufficiently
precise and delimiting to give the psychologist much guidance
in identifying them. What precisely is the hallmark of a dynamically significant pattern of behavior? Are there temporal
sequences of functioning that can be definitely discarded as
not significant? How long or short can a proceeding be? The
questions are many, as Murray has not progressed far in his
admittedly difficult but certainly worthwhile task.

At the moment, the theories of Allport, Maslow, and Murray all rely heavily upon the heterogeneous, sometimes vague, meanings and distinctions concerning functioning that are learned by virtue of membership in our culture. This lack of complete, explicit data specification makes for inconsistency in application of the theories, and renders precise prediction virtually impossible. Although none of these theorists has provided sufficient data specification, one can get a further sense of the kinds of data that are likely to be important from a consideration of the actual concepts and propositions of the theories.

The Relatively Concrete Concepts of Personality

Personality theories, as any others, are constituted of various concepts that are clarified and interrelated by the statements in which they appear. Attention will first be given to the simpler, more concrete concepts and their interrelationships.

Allport's basic concept, the *personal disposition,* is defined as

a generalized neuropsychic structure (peculiar to the individual), with the capacity to render many stimuli functionally equivalent, and to initiate and guide consistent (equivalent) forms of adaptive and stylistic behavior. (Allport, 1961, p. 373)

The concept that has equivalent importance in Murray's theory is the *need,* considered to be

a construct (a convenient fiction or hypothetical concept) which stands for a force . . . in the brain region, a force which organizes perception, apperception, intellection, conation, and action in such a way as to transform in a certain direction an existing, unsatisfying situation. A need is sometimes provoked directly by internal processes of a certain kind . . . but, more frequently (when in a state of readiness) by the occurrence of one of a few commonly effective press. (Murray, 1938, pp. 123–24)

Maslow also used the *need* concept, referring by it to organismic requirements, dynamic forces expressing human goals,
which organize and direct behavior toward gratifications
(Maslow, 1954). These needs are considered "instinctoid,"
or similar to instincts, in that they are universal to man in
the sense of being not only species wide but also species specific. Although rooted in the organic nature of man, the
needs are not full-fledged instincts (being only instinctoid)
because each need can be expressed and satisfied in many
different ways.

In gaining greater understanding of these three basic concepts, it is useful to compare them for their attributed uniqueness, neurophysiological substrate, effects upon functioning,
and susceptibility to arousal.

UNIQUENESS

Allport believes that each personal disposition is unique to
the individual studies; Murray feels more than one person
can possess a particular need. In Maslow's framework, each
need is present in every member of the human species,
though expressions of needs may vary from person to person.
Prepotent needs, like all the basic needs, account for similarities across different people, on one level; on another level,
they lead to unique differences among people. Maslow distinguishes between the multiplicity of instrumental strategies
and the specific conscious desires that partly define the motives represented in the basic needs from the fundamental
goals or satisfactions that remain constant through all the
flux. Maslow did not concentrate on any listing of drives ("in
the ordinary sense of instigation") but on the need's capacity
to organize diverse behaviors into a unified pattern. In the
average person, the basic needs are not so much directly observed, but conceptually derived from the multiplicity of specific desires. Thus the effects of needs upon functioning may
be unique from one person to another, behaviorally, but

they represent ultimate ends or goals, certain need-satisfactions that are constant ends in themselves.

Allport (1961, p. 349) included in his theory of uniqueness the less important concept of *common trait* to account for the similarities stemming from the possession of a common human nature and a common culture. But the common trait, though an admissable and useful concept, is an abstraction arrived at by generalizing across people, and hence necessarily misses the actual dispositions of each individual to some degree. The real personality emerges only when personal dispositions are assessed, and this requires intensive study of an individual's past, present, and anticipated future functioning, through the use of such techniques as the case history and content analysis of personal documents (Allport, 1961, pp. 367–69; 1962). While Murray agrees upon the usefulness of such methods of diagnosis, he will readily generalize across people in the assessment of needs. It is this difference, probably more than any other, that has permitted Murray to compile lists of typical needs that can guide the diagnostic efforts of the investigator. In contrast, Allport has been unwilling to narrow the number of dispositions any further than the combinations that would be possible using the 18,000 or so common trait names in the English language (Allport and Odbert, 1936).

NEUROPHYSIOLOGICAL SUBSTRATE

Allport's personal disposition is considered a neuropsychic structure, Murray's need is represented as a force in the brain region, and Maslow described needs as instinctoid. All three theorists presume that their respective concepts refer to entities that are real not only psychologically but physiologically as well. Murray's statement of the hypothetical quality of the need is best interpreted as careful recognition that the inference a theorist always makes in specifying a concept defines the risk he takes of misinterpreting the actual state of affairs.

Both Allport (1961, p. 28) and Murray (1938, p. 45; 1968, pp. 6–7) believe that the brain is the only possible locus of personality, because only the brain is neuroanatomically and neurophysiologically suited to play the necessary integrative role. But while specification of the brain as the neurophysiological substrate of personal dispositions seems sufficient for Allport, Murray suggests further that needs may have sources outside of the brain, even though they are not categorizable as needs at all unless they are represented at the brain level as well. Thus, Murray (1954, pp. 13–21) has sometimes classified needs as having the source in the viscera, in the requirements of society or in the requirements of central nervous tissue itself. Allport's personal dispositions are considered so heavily psychological that little more appears necessary to say about them neurologically except that they have representation in the brain. Maslow's position is much like that of Murray, but with greater reliance upon somatic, visceral sources of needs, and less insistence on the importance of brain representation. Maslow talked of needs as instinctoid because he believed that they are the remnants in the human of the animal instincts appearing lower on the phylogenetic scale. The instinctoid, or human, needs are less insistent and fixed than outright instincts, but share with them the property of arising from the complex whole that is the body. According to Maslow (1954, Chapter 4), the person's constitution, temperament, nervous system, and endocrine system and all their capacities constitute the structure out of which needs emerge.

Even though Maslow and Murray have elaborated their views a little more than did Allport, it must be concluded that the neurophysiological emphasis of the three theorists, though worthwhile as a potential source of integration of knowledge from disparate fields of psychology, is at present little more than a signpost indicating an important direction for study.

EFFECTS UPON FUNCTIONING

The major effects of both dispositions and needs upon functioning are to produce perceptions, interpretations, feelings, and actions that are equivalent in terms of meaning or purpose. In discussing the influence of a personal disposition, Allport (1961, p. 322) develops the following example. While Russians, college professors, liberals, peace organizations, and anti-segregationists may seem different to many observers, to a person with the disposition *fear of communism* all these stimulus configurations may be equivalent in their perceived communist properties. Such a disposition also engenders response sequences that are equivalent in their function of reducing the perceived threat of communism. The individual might advocate war with the Russians, be suspicious of teachers, vote for extreme right wing persons and policies, join the Ku Klux Klan or the John Birch Society, and so forth. Stimulus and response equivalences are diagnosed on the basis of perceived meanings and related coping behavior, rather than on any necessarily obvious similarities. Yet one suspects, from the very example itself, that the stimuli that can be perceived equivalently by a person with a particular disposition are not unlimited. They probably share some core of denotative or connotative meaning in the general culture to which such an individual's perceptual processes have become particularly sensitive. That individual overlooks all other possible meanings of the stimuli and responds consistently with his selective perception. An explication of such matters would certainly make the personal disposition concept more concrete and usable.

To Murray, the diagnosis of particular needs requires observation of equivalences of meaning in the individual's (1) initiating or reacting inner state, (2) perception of the external situation, (3) imagined goal or aim, (4) directionality of concomitant movements and words, and (5) produced effect, if any (Murray, 1954, pp. 456–63). Although the description is somewhat different from that used by Allport, the emphasis upon classing certain perceptual, cognitive, affective, and actional characteristics together on the basis of their function or meaning is largely the same. Unlike Allport, however, Murray (1954, p. 459) emphasizes the importance of a detailed description of the objective as well as the subjective features of a stimulus situation. Any discrepancy of correspondence between the first of these, called the *alpha situation,* and the second, called the *beta situation,* is an important clue to an identification of the existing needs, and even to such matters as their intensity and selectivity.

The general agreement of Maslow with the two other theorists about effects upon functioning is well exemplified by his statement that

> . . . not only does the need organize its action possibilities, so to speak, in the most efficient way feasible and with a great deal of variation, but it organizes and even creates the external reality. (Maslow, 1954, p. 74)

This emphasis on needs as organizing and creating action possibilities and external realities is strikingly similar to Allport's idea that dispositions render stimuli and responses functionally equivalent. This general theme of functional equivalence of objectively different stimuli and responses expresses the holistic emphasis of all three theorists even at the level of their most concrete concepts of personality. Needs and dispositions must be understood as serving an organizing and integrating role in life, and cannot be defined in terms of some invariant and simple set of responses or environmental pressure. Although Maslow uses the need concept, as does Murray, Maslow described his form of the concept in a much more general, perhaps ambiguous fashion than does Murray. Nowhere in Maslow's writing is there concern with analysing the *particular* ways in which needs affect functioning by rendering perception, action, thoughts, and feelings functionally equivalent. In addition, although Maslow agrees with Murray that needs can be provoked by external pressures, Maslow does not give detailed discussion to presses, emphasizing instead "fundamental needs which are relatively constant and independent of the particular situation in which the organism finds itself" (Maslow, 1954, p. 74). The organism usually behaves as an integrated whole. To Maslow, the proper concern is with motivation theory, not behavior theory; the object of study is in "the understanding of the nature of the constancy of the organism" rather than in an "understanding of the world it lives in." Although situational determinants are not meant to be excluded from concern, Maslow emphasizes the organism's aims and tasks as the central focus.

From the holistic, integrative emphasis of both the disposition and need concepts, it is understandable to find that, although these concepts include properties usually identified with attitudes and habits, they are not as narrow in purpose or specific action as these. Although there are attitudinal features in many dispositions and needs, these concepts are not so closely tied to specific sets of objects as is the attitude. Although there are habitual modes of behaving included in many dispositions and needs, these concepts do not imply the rigid response repetition of the habit.

There seems to be a difference between the need and disposition concepts in the degree to which they are motivational. For need, the equivalences of functioning are closely tied to the effect the individual is trying to achieve, which might be called the "why" of behavior. Disposition seems to give a larger place to the "what" and "how" of behavior. But care must be taken not to exaggerate this difference. Allport considers the usual distinction between dynamic and structural units of personality to be inapplicable. He believes all personal dispositions to be motivational to some degree in that they cause behavior (Allport, 1961, p. 370). Those dispositions involving greater or less *intention* have been called *dynamic* and *stylistic,* respectively (ibid., pp. 222–25). Murray (1938, pp. 96–101) includes qualities of style or form (the "what" and "how" of functioning) in his concept of need, calling them *actones.* In a fashion similar to Allport, Maslow (1954, p. 180) distinguished between *coping* (motivated) behavior, which is directed toward the achievement of ends, and *expressive* ("useless") behavior, which is an end in itself.

There is another slight difference in emphasis between disposition and need in the thinking of the three theorists. Allport's concept refers more concretely to stimulus and response equivalences, while the concepts relied upon by Murray and Maslow stress directional tension more than the specifics of its expression. Looked at from this point of view, need is probably less analogous to disposition than is the concept of need-integrate in Murray's system (1938, pp. 109–110), and *canalization* in Maslow's system (1954, p. 138). The need-integrate concept refers not only to directional tension but also to the specific object cathexes and characteristic actones that become grafted to it through learning accomplished in the course of repeated expression of the need. Murray says that "traces (images) of cathected objects in familiar settings become integrated in the mind with the needs and emotions which they customarily excite, as well as with images of preferred modes. . . . The integrate may enter consciousness as a fantasy or plan of action, or, under appropriate circumstances, it may be objectified, in which case it can be operationally defined as a reaction pattern that is evoked by certain conditions" (Murray, 1938, p. 110). Maslow's (1954, p. 139) similar emphasis on canalization refers to the establishment of stable preferences for certain kinds of objects for satisfying needs. Need-canalization involves learning which objects are intrinsically proper gratifications and which objects are not.

SUSCEPTIBILITY TO AROUSAL

Allport gives little formal role in his theory to the arousal of personal dispositions by particular features of the external situation. Dispositions are not aroused; rather, they exist continuously, having an ongoing effect upon functioning that is consistent in magnitude with their intensity and centrality. Although Maslow used the need concept, his emphasis is similar to that of Allport. According to Maslow, "motivation is a constant, never-ending, fluctuating and complex process and it is an almost universal characteristic of practically every organismic state of affairs" (Maslow, 1954, p. 69). This ubiquitousness of needs is considered to stem from their source in the body as an organic system. But it is true that Maslow considered need intensity to subside once gratification has been achieved. So, while not triggered by external events, needs do wax and wane depending upon levels of gratification. Although Murray agrees that need intensity is a function of level of gratification, he disagrees in emphasis with both Allport and Maslow by theorizing that the triggering action of some perceived situational pressure is necessary in order for the need to become an active determinant of functioning. The subjectively experienced pressure is called *beta press,* and is to be distinguished from the objective pressure, or *alpha press* (Murray, 1938, pp. 115–23).

Murray (1938, p. 123) has found an interactional unit, the *thema,* or combination of a need and press, to be basic for the psychologist. It is the thema that determines specific proceedings. Murray is unclear as to whether the press component of the thema refers to the individual's own perception of the situation or to its objective features. If the beta perceived press is intended, then the thema may be more directly analogous to the personal disposition than is the need. The thema and the alpha (objective) press, taken together, would suggest that Murray believes clarification of the objective features of the situation that are selected for perception by the individual possessing a particular need is important for precise explanation and prediction. But it may be the alpha press that is considered to form part of the thema. This seems possible because, as has been shown, the need and need-integrate concepts already include certain influences upon perception, suggesting that the beta press would be superfluous as a component of the thema. If the alpha press is intended, then Murray seems to be less phenomenological and more concerned with reactivity than is Allport and Maslow. If both alpha and beta press are to be included, Murray must specify the different role of each in the thema.

CLASSIFICATIONS

Allport, Maslow, and Murray have all offered classifications associated with their concepts, so that one may know what sorts of dispositions and needs are supposed to exist. One classification offered by Allport (1961, p. 365) involves the pervasiveness and consistency with which personal dispositions influence functioning. Distinctions are made along these lines between cardinal, central, and secondary dispositions. The first, if they exist in a personality, will set the pattern of an individual's life; the second, possessed by virtually all people, are significant stabilizing features of functioning; and the third are of relatively transient importance. Another principle of classification offered by Allport is less clear, though it bears some resemblance to the one just described. This classification refers to the degree to which a disposition is at the core of an individual's being (Allport, 1961, p. 264). The application of this principle leads to the Lewinian distinction between the genotypical and phenotypical disposition; the latter, though it involves some consistency in functioning, being less a reflection of the essential nature of the personality than is the former. From Allport's discussion it is not entirely clear what difference there is between genotypical and cardinal dispositions and between phenotypical and central dispositions.

Murray has experimented over the years with a number of apparently overlapping classifications of types and qualities of needs. One classification takes into account the degree to which the individual's aim in his activity is intrinsic or extrinsic to the form of that activity. This leads to the distinction between *activity needs* and *effect needs*. Activity needs, or tendencies to "engage in a certain kind of activity for its own sake" (Murray, 1954, p. 445), are subdivided into *process needs,* involving performance, or action, for the sheer pleasure to be derived from the exercise of available functions, and *mode needs,* which are satisfied by the excellence of activity rather than its mere occurrence (ibid., p. 446). Effect needs are marked by attempts to bring about a particular desired effect or goal which is extrinsic to the activity engaged in, that activity serving an instrumental purpose (Murray and Kluckhohn, 1956, p. 15). Although Murray is one of the few to conceptualize activity for its own sake, he has given most of his attention to effect needs.

Another classificatory attempt offered by Murray seems to emphasize the origin of the need, and, hence, the particular direction of activity that it imposes. In this attempt, *mental, viscerogenic,* and *socio-relational needs* are distinguished (Murray, 1954, pp. 445–52; Murray and Kluckhohn, 1956, pp. 13–21). The well-known viscerogenic needs stem from tissue requirements and have very specific, easily recognizable goals. The mental needs are usually overlooked; they stem from the fact that "the human mind is inherently a transforming, creating, and representing organ; its function is to make symbols for things, to combine and recombine these symbols incessantly, and to communicate the most interesting of the combinations in a variety of languages, discursive (referential, scientific) and expressive (emotive, artistic)" (Murray and Kluckhohn, 1956, p. 16). As the viscera have certain requirements, so too does the mind, and both sets of requirements stem from the nature of man. Mental needs do not have very specific goal states. Socio-relational needs arise from the inherently social nature of man (Murray, 1959, pp. 47–57) and include such specific dispositions as the *need for roleship,* the need "to become and to remain an accepted and respected, differentiated and integrated part of a congenial, functioning group, the collective purposes of which are congruent with the individual's ideals" (Murray, 1954, pp. 451–52). As described, the need for roleship seems to imply particular learning produced by the individual's experiences against the ever present background of his inherent socio-relational nature. There are probably specific forms of each of the types of inherent needs that develop through specific learning.

In one discussion of classifications, Murray (1954, pp. 445–52) includes two other types of needs that presumably cut across the mental, viscerogenic, and socio-relational, and seem to emphasize adient and abient tendencies. These are *creative needs,* which aim at the construction of new and useful thoughts and objects, and *negative needs,* which aim at the avoidance or termination of unpleasant, noxious conditions.

An early typology distinguishes what are primarily effect needs, of a mental, viscerogenic, and socio-relational variety, on the basis of a much more fine-grained consideration of goals (Murray, 1938, pp. 152–226). This attempt includes such familiar concepts as *n* achievement, *n* affiliation, and other needs that are considered to be of a psychogenic or learned variety along with those that are presumably innate. Extensive behavior descriptions are included in an effort to define the needs operationally.

Added to these various classifications of personality are distinctions between certain qualities that needs may possess. Needs can be proactive or reactive, diffuse or focal, latent or overt, conscious or unconscious (Murray, 1938, pp. 111–15; 1954, pp. 447–50).

Maslow also distinguishes several types of needs, though

he has been more consistent over the years in the bases upon which he drew distinctions than Murray has been. The basic need distinctions for Maslow (1954, Chapter 8) is between *higher* and *lower* needs. The lower needs reflect little more than the biological requirements of the organism for physical survival, and do not distinguish the human being from other animals. In contrast, the higher needs reflect biological potentialities rather than requirements, and do not insure physical survival so much as enrich life in psychological and social ways. Needless to say, the higher needs are unique to man, finding no more than rudimentary expression, if that, at lower phylogenetic levels. In a later discussion, Maslow (1955) considered higher needs to represent *growth motivation* and lower needs to represent *deprivation motivation*. Deprivation motivation refers to urges to strive for goal states, presently unachieved, that are necessary in order to ease the pain and discomfort caused by their absence. The aim of deprivation motivation is to decrease the organismic tension built up through deficit states that represent deviations from homeostatic, physiological balance. Organismic survival requires nutritional substances, and hence, when food (or some other nutrient) has not been ingested for a while, visceral organ activity produces a rising tension level, experienced psychologically as hunger, which precipitates instrumental actions designed to reach the goal state. The goal state is satiation, which is considered the normal, homeostatic state, characterized as tensionless.

In contrast to deprivation motivation, growth motivation, which Maslow claims has not been adequately recognized in the past, refers to urgings to enrich living, to enlarge experience, because to do so increases our delight at being alive. Growth motivation does not involve the repairing of deficits so much as the expansion of horizons. Its goal states, if they exist at all, are very general in nature. There is no starting point of sharp discomfort that must be eased, and growth motivation does not aim at the reduction of tension so much as at its actual increase. Satisfaction has to do with realization of capabilities or ideals, through a process whereby the organism becomes more complex, differentiated, and potent. Such an enlargement of the organism seems to require, if anything, that satisfaction go hand in hand with tension increase.

Maslow's distinction between growth and deprivation motivation is similar to that drawn by Murray between activity and effect needs. Maslow's distinction also bears some more general similarity to Allport's separation of cardinal, central, and secondary dispositions in that cardinal dispositions, like growth motivation, push the person so much in the direction of greater complexity and differentiation that they could hardly be consistent with anything but tension increase. Indeed, as a later section of this book will document, Allport and Maslow were in close agreement in separating the functioning of the person into those things in which he seeks lowered tension and is most like lower animals and those things in which he welcomes tension increase and is most uniquely human.

In an attempt to be even more concrete, Maslow subdivided the categories of higher (growth) and lower (deprivation) needs, though he was not always entirely consistent in his writings on the number of such subdivisions and the names of the ensuing categories (Maslow, 1954, pp. 147–50). It is fair to say, after threading one's way through these ambiguities, that Maslow considered the following categories: *physiological needs, safety needs, needs for belongingness and love, esteem needs, need for self-actualization,* and *need for cognitive understanding.* Although it is not entirely clear where the list of categories is definitively divided into higher (growth) and lower (deprivation) needs, Maslow was consistent in considering at least the need for self-actualization and the need for cognitive understanding as higher (Maslow, 1951, 1954, 1962). The other needs can therefore probably be considered lower. Included under physiological needs are such well-known requirements as that for food, water, and air; safety needs refer essentially to the avoidance of pain and physical damage through external forces; needs for belongingness and love concern the general characteristic of living things to feel secure when in close, intimate contact with other organisms. In referring to esteem needs, recognition is given to the importance of having status and acceptance in one's group. The need for self-actualization refers to the natural tendency of the human to act in a manner expressive of his potentialities and capabilities, whatever they may be. The need for cognitive understanding indicates that humans have an inborn push toward awareness, consciousness of themselves and the external world, and an appreciation of meaning.

Finally, Maslow endorsed, in a very general way, some of the qualities of needs mentioned more explicitly by Murray. Of these qualities, the one most relevant to Maslow's thinking is the distinction between conscious and unconscious needs. Obviously, some needs, like that for cognitive understanding, aim at consciousness, but other needs do not. Indeed, according to Maslow, the lower needs may even be typically unconscious.

The concepts of need and personal disposition are heterogeneous in that they refer to many observationally different aspects of functioning. Hence, any classifications of types or qualities of these general entities that can be provided might increase their usability. And yet, with the few exceptions mentioned above, Allport did not attempt to delineate any of the relatively general aspects of personal dispositions that might lead to clarifying comparisons. His strong emphasis upon the uniqueness of each disposition undoubtedly inhibits any extensive attempt to classify, even though such an emphasis does not necessarily preclude limited progress along these lines. Particular features of a disposition may be similar to those of others without jeopardizing the uniqueness of that disposition in its totality. Further, as disposition is a concept referring directly to behavior, its operational definition would seem indispensable to consistency of usage from one investigator to another, yet none is given, most likely because the emphasis upon uniqueness seems to render such a definition fruitless if not impossible before actual diagnosis is made. Human functioning is complex enough so that, without benefit of more concrete guide lines, stimulus and response equivalences can be found at many different levels and in many different ways. Each investigator is thrown completely upon his own artistry in each diagnosis of a dispostion. He cannot derive much assistance from the diagnoses of other investigators, or from his own prior diagnoses, nor can he be entirely sure that he is using the concept in the manner Allport may have intended.

Although Murray also believes in individuality, he has found it possible to attempt extensive classification and operational definition because the need is more of a nomothetic concept than is the disposition. Probably in the total array of a person's needs, rather than in each individual need, Murray best pinpoints individuality, but his classificatory and definitional attempts are only of partial assistance in making the concept more concrete and usable.

Murray's writing yields a bewildering array of overlapping classifications of needs. It is difficult to come by any one authoritative typology. Murray has not addressed himself to the relationships between the available schemes in sufficient detail to make his thinking perfectly clear. While his shifting distinctions and the resulting ambiguities probably represent the difficulty of conceptualizing human complexities, they also stem from the extreme heterogeneity of functioning subsumed by the need concept (Fiske, 1963). Each need can be manifested in many internal and external ways, and Murray wishes to consider a great number of needs and types of needs. Not surprisingly, the influences upon functioning attributed to any particular need tends to overlap with the presumed manifestations of other needs. Reasoning from behavioral observations to a great number and variety of needs also precipitates a large and heterogeneous mass of assumed organismic requirements. No wonder finding a basis for classifying needs that will keep them reasonably distinct in theory and in practice is difficult. Given the inherent heterogeneity of his need concept, Murray may be attempting a fineness of distinction between exemplars of the concept that is too great for classificatory neatness and clarity.

Such over refinement of a basically heterogeneous concept should make for considerable difficulty in using or applying need analysis. A look at the detailed operational descriptions for each of the psychogenic needs is not reassuring on this score. One suspects the great difficulty of making the fine distinctions in meaning that are required in order to distinguish one need from another. This difficulty is bound to be compounded in the typical research situation, where the investigator finds available only some, rather than all, of the possible manifestations of needs. It is understandable that in a major attempt to employ Murray's (1938) typology, it was necessary to reach the diagnosis of particular needs by majority vote of a group of skilled investigators after considerable debate concerning their observations.

Perhaps because of these problems in using and applying need analysis, Murray has moved in the direction of substituting the *value-vector* concept for the need (Murray, 1954, pp. 463–64). The vector principle refers to the nature of the directionality shown by behavior (for example, rejection, acquisition, construction). The value principle refers to the ideals that are important to people (for example, knowledge, beauty, authority). A value-vector matrix is compiled in diagnosing what each person believes is worthwhile, and the particular ways in which he moves to make those beliefs an actuality. At this early stage in its use, the value-vector system seems to involve less heterogeneity and fewer organismic assumptions than does the need system. The values and vectors currently listed are simple enough and few enough so that it should be more possible to reach agreement among investigators on their identification in functioning.

Although Maslow also relied upon the need concept, it may seem as if he avoided the problems of ambiguity criticized in Murray. After all, did not Maslow provide a rather understandable classification of needs, without an overly precise specification of the behavioral implications of needs that would doom attempts at diagnosis? Remember however, that Murray seriously attempted to delineate his need concept concretely enough so that it could be used in the diagnosis of behavior, whereas Maslow was content with a much more general level of theorizing. Even such subcategories in Maslow's scheme as physiological and esteem needs refer to sets of clustered needs—sets that are essentially unspecified. Even if the sets were specified, however, it would still be necessary to become concrete about their various expressions in behavior in order to have any way of actually using Maslow's position. Once this were done, it is likely that the ambiguities found in Murray due to the over refinement of an inherently heterogeneous concept would rise to plague Maslow as well. It is unwarranted to afford Maslow more credit merely because he may have avoided a difficulty inherent in his approach by not developing his concept as far as necessary in order for it to be useful in empirical endeavor.

Interrelationships Between the Relatively Concrete Concepts

Consideration of the interrelationships between personal dispositions on the one hand and needs on the other suggests that both Allport and Murray favor a hierarchical organization. Thus, Allport distinguishes between cardinal, central, and secondary dispositions on the basis of their generality and consistency. With somewhat similar intent, Murray includes the concepts of *unity-thema,* a need-press combination that is pervasive because it has been formed early in life (Murray, 1938, pp. 604–605) and *pre-potency,* or the degree to which a need takes precedence over others when it is aroused (Murray, 1954, p. 452). Also relevant is Murray's (1938, pp. 86–88) idea of *subsidiation,* whereby less potent needs can become instrumental to the satisfaction of other needs.

Both Allport and Murray recognize that a single course of action may actually reflect the operation of more than one disposition or need. Thus Allport (1961, p. 377) employs the concept of *convergence* and Murray (1938, p. 86) includes *fusion* of needs. Both theorists also recognize that dispositions or needs can be in conflict with each other. This idea is of greatest importance to Murray (1938, pp. 88–89).

In order for these statements concerning the interrelationships between personal dispositions and needs to be usable, it is necessary to delineate the conditions under which the various interrelational concepts hold. When, and under what specific conditions, do fusion, convergence, and subsidiation occur? What makes a disposition become cardinal rather than central? It can be seen that there is much theoretical work to be done in explicating the ways in which dispositions or needs are related to each other.

Although Maslow emphasized holism, and would therefore be in general agreement with Allport and Murray, he actually offered no specific concepts such as those mentioned above to explain the joint action of several needs. He did, however, make a very important statement of another sort concerning the interrelationship of needs. Maslow believes that the sets of needs previously described are arranged in a hierarchical order, starting with physiological needs at the bottom and progressing through safety needs, to needs for belongingness and love, to esteem needs, to the need for self-actualization, to the need for cognitive understanding, which stands at the top of the hierarchy. The nature of the interrelationship among these sets of needs is that those lower in the hierarchy must be satisfied to a substantial degree before those situated higher up can emerge strongly. In other words, one will only feel the need for belongingness and love after physiological and safety needs are satisfied, and the need for self-actualization will provoke relevant actions only after needs up to and including those for esteem have been successfully expressed.

Maslow based this position on the assumption that the lower a need on the hierarchy the greater is its *prepotency.*

> Thus the safety need is stronger than the love need, because it dominates the organism in various demonstrable ways when both needs are frustrated. In this sense the physiological needs (which are themselves ordered in a subhierarchy) are stronger than the safety needs, which are stronger than the love needs, which in turn are stronger than the esteem needs, which are stronger than those idiosyncratic needs which we have called the need for self-actualization. (Maslow, 1954, pp. 146–47)

Maslow detailed 16 comparisons between higher and lower needs in an attempt to be more specific about the meaning of difference in prepotency (Maslow, 1954, pp. 147–50). Although many of the differences are obvious, and seem to overlap, some are important enough to set down here. Of two needs differing in position on the hierarchy, the higher is weaker than the lower because the higher (1) is a later phylogenetic or evolutionary development, (2) is later in ontogenetic development, (3) is less imperative for sheer survival, (4) can permit of more postponement of gratification, and (5) is more likely to disappear permanently.

The clear implication of Maslow's position is that the further up the hierarchy of needs a person is able to go, the more individuality, humanness, and psychological health he will have. In order to proceed to the life pursuits expressive of a particular set of needs on the hierarchy, all sets of needs lower than it must have been substantially satisfied, and in order for the most vigorous mental health to be achieved, one must have had all of the physiological, safety, love, and esteem needs met. Clearly, this means that the person must be nurtured, loved, and respected, in order to amount to much. As Maddi (1968, pp. 87–88) has suggested, this viewpoint, however humanistic it may be, can be criticized by scrutinizing the lives of great men. There are countless examples of people (for example, Galileo, Michelangelo, James Baldwin) who were significantly creative in spite of early lives that hardly included much nurturance, love, and respect. The criticism can be carried even further, for an implication of Maslow's position is that when lower needs are frustrated at any point in time—not simply in childhood—there ought to be a concomitant temporary decrease in vigorous self-actualization and cognitive understanding. Once again, however, there are many contradictory examples to be found in the lives of great men (Maddi, 1968, pp. 87–88). By way of merest example, think of the obstacles (frustration of safety and esteem needs) to Jesus Christ's creativity, and the continuous physical pain (frustration of safety needs) under which Toulouse-Lautrec labored, and the mental anguish (frustration of needs for belongingness and love and for esteem) endured by Van Gogh.

Maslow might respond to this criticism by saying that his position is accurate in general, regardless of the fact that one can point to exceptions. For most people, he might argue, the realization of potentialities requires the prior satisfaction of survival needs. There will always be a few people, presumably, who are so extraordinary that their lives will be creative and healthy whether or not they are nurtured. In discussing the question of the degree of fixity of the hierarchy of the basic needs as well as reversals in the hierarchy, Maslow hastily recognizes that higher-level needs such as creativeness "might appear not as self-actualization released by basic satisfaction, but in spite of lack of basic satisfaction" (Maslow, 1954, p. 98). Maslow might want to suggest that these people could have been even greater if their survival needs had achieved more satisfaction. While this is a plausible counterargument, it implies the need for changes in Maslow's formulation that might be more far reaching than is immediately apparent.

3

The Formal Theories: Relatively General Concepts

Allport, Maslow, and Murray utilize concepts that are at a higher level of generality and complexity than need or personal disposition. In these very general concepts, even more than in the relatively concrete ones, we can discern the assumptions that the three theorists have made concerning the nature of man. By and large, the portions of their theories to be considered here are less clearly delineated than those in the previous section; hence it will not be profitable to attempt the detail of presentation and comparison that was possible earlier.

Id, Superego, Ego

Murray considers the *establishments* of personality to be the *id, superego, ego-ideal,* and *ego* (Murray, 1938, pp. 134–41; Murray and Kluckhohn, 1956, pp. 23–28). Although these are familiar concepts, he has elaborated their meaning from the original Freudian usage. The id, though still a repository of innate dynamic tendencies alone, contains not only self-seeking, destructive impulses but more acceptable tendencies as well. Among the latter are "respiration, ingestion of food, defecation, expressions of affection, endeavors to master the environment, and so forth. . . . The id is evidently the breed-

ing ground of love and worship, as well as of the novel imaginations which are eventually applauded, instituted, and cherished by society" (Murray and Kluckhohn, 1956, p. 24).
Murray gives the status of innate tendencies to some valuable
qualities that Freud would have explained as involving the
impact of the defenses upon unacceptable impulses. Murray's
conceptualization of the id reflects his assumption of the basically visceral, mental, social, and growth-oriented nature of
man. The id can vary in strength from person to person, according presumably to the biological and physiological features of each organism. Very strong id tendencies can be inferred from intense energy of zest, needs and appetites, emotions, and imagination (ibid., p. 26).

Murray utilizes the superego concept to refer to the internal
representation of the value system of an individual's society,
in terms of which he judges and disciplines himself and others
(Murray and Kluckhohn, 1956, pp. 26–28). He has elaborated upon the concept as used by Freud by recognizing the
determining influences of such extra-parental factors as peer
group pressures, literature, and the like. One of the major
functions of the superego is to censor expressions of id impulses that are unacceptable to society, both for the individual
himself and for others with whom he comes in contact. The
ego-ideal is a gradually developing, envisaged ideal self which
guides the ego, when that personality component becomes
sufficiently differentiated and integrated, in arbitrating between emotional impulses from the id and superego imperatives (ibid., p. 28). In order to guide effectively, the ego-ideal
must stay within the organism's potentialities. If the ego-ideal
is entirely divorced from the superego, the individual will very
likely be trying to become something unacceptable to society.
Murray's discussion of the superego and the id indicates that
he provides more latitude for their alteration and change in
the years subsequent to childhood than did Freud.

Perhaps the major elaboration made by Murray on Freud's scheme is in the conceptualization of the ego. To be sure, the ego is the rational and "differentiated governing establishment of personality" (Murray and Kluckhohn, 1956, p. 26), and functions to block and temper the expression of id impulses that are unacceptable to society and the superego through the employment of defenses. But Murray accords the ego a much more important, active role in determining the individual's functioning and precipitating psychological growth. It arranges, schedules, controls, and otherwise facilitates and promotes the expression of the socially-valued id impulses. It includes capacities or abilities that are indispensable not only to adequate survival but also to excellence of living. A perusal of those abilities possessed by a strong, effective ego will show clearly the importance of this concept to Murray (ibid., pp. 24–26). The *perceptual* and *apperceptual* abilities tend toward external and internal objectivity or veridicality, and long apperception span or time perspective. The *intellectual abilities* are concentration and the conjunctivity and referentiality of thought and speech. The *conative abilities* are will power, conjunctivity of action, resolution of conflicts, selectivity in the impulses expressed and the social pressures responded to, initiative and self-sufficiency, responsibility for collective action, adherence to resolutions and agreements, and absence of psychopathological symptoms.

Through the ego functions characterized by Murray, the *schedules* for the orderly expression of contiguously aroused needs (Murray and Kluckhohn, 1956, pp. 38–39) and the *serial programs,* which insure a gradual movement toward the achievement of complex goals (ibid., p. 37), come about. The schedules and serial programs also contribute largely to the proactive flavor of the proceedings and serials constituting an individual's functioning. Ideally, this organizing action of the ego is rendered more effective through being interrelated with the superego's internalized standards of acceptability in the time, place, and mode of expression of dynamic tendencies.

Proprium

Turning to Allport's more complex concepts of personality, we find that the closest he came to anything like the id—and it is not very close—is the belief that organismic features, determined largely by biological factors such as temperament, serve to impart certain limits to the possible development of personality. The superordinate concept in Allport's system is the *proprium,* which serves an organizing and integrating role and provides an impetus to psychological growth. In an attempt to avoid the misunderstandings and bitterness that have attended concepts of self in psychology, Allport initially tried to conceptualize the proprium as a set of ongoing functions, without paying much attention to structural substance (Allport, 1955, pp. 41–56). In a later work, Allport more clearly discusses function as implying structure, even though he retains emphasis upon function. The functions of the proprium are *sense of body, self-identity, self-esteem, self-extension,* rational coping, self-image, and *propriate striving* (Allport, 1961, pp. 110–38). Allport considers these the vital portions of personality because they have in common a phenomenal warmth and sense of importance to the individual and thus permeate his life. Although the functions of the proprium are ongoing, they are by no means unchanging. Instead, they are modified throughout life, predominantly in the direction of greater differentiation and integration, or growth.

There are many similarities in general emphasis between Allport's proprium and Murray's ego. Both broad categories of personality produce or reflect organization, rationality, consistency, future orientation, planfulness, self-expression, cognitive complexity, and adaptability. Both theorists (Allport, 1955, pp. 56–59; Murray and Kluckhohn, 1956, pp. 24–26, 33–49) believe that the various functions or abilities fuse or act in interdependence with one another. It does not seem fruitful at this time to attempt any more precise, detailed comparison of the proprium and ego, because the theorists have not yet delineated the nature and actions of these personality components with any great degree of specificity.

Murray's concept of personality appears to be more heterogeneous than does Allport's. One is struck by the impression that the ego includes functions or abilities that are at different levels of generality and meaning. In deciding upon the abilities to be included, Murray seems to rely primarily upon his own estimate of those which have been most useful to man. In contrast, Allport considers only functions that are assumed to be actually experienced by individuals as important, central parts of them (Allport, 1955, pp. 39–40). Murray's less restrictive, perhaps less differentiated, criterion has permitted the juxtaposition of strange bedfellows. Seemingly basic organismic capacities such as concentration and long apperceptive span are included together with such characteristics as freedom from psychopathological symptoms, a condition which is more a judgment about the soundness of functioning than a statement about basic ability. Certainly, Allport did not escape the inclusion of functions at different levels of generality and meaning—witness his grouping of bodily sense and propriate striving—but his adherence to the requirement of phenomenal importance makes the proprium seem more unified than Murray's ego.

Allport, in making a short list of propriate functions applying to sound adults, departs from his previously extreme idiographic position. From the point of view of adding precise meaning to, and increasing the usability of, his theory, this seems a worthwhile departure, all the more because the propriate functions are sufficiently devoid of specific content to permit considerable room for individuality in the particular styles of behavior that can be identified as developing out of a propriate orientation toward living.

Both Allport and Murray intend to delineate universalistic aspects of personality in postulating their relatively general concepts. All persons are believed to have propriums, ids, egos, and superegos. And while it is true that Allport and Murray do consider the content of these universalistic features of personality, they do not do so for reasons of discussing the differences among people, or even the special qualities that make a person just who he is. Although Allport and Murray value individuality, their formal theories do not put much emphasis on it. But Murray does come close to the beginning of such an emphasis when he discusses personality complexes, such as the claustral, oral, and anal types. This will be discussed later.

Syndromes

The major thrust of Maslow's thinking regarding relatively general features of personality is in the direction of identifying the particular organizations of personality that make a person just who he is, and his life just what it is. Maslow sometimes called these organized wholes *syndromes,* and sometimes *types* (Maslow, 1954, pp. 31–36). His emphasis is clearly on understanding the interrelationship and mutual influence of just those expressions of the needs mentioned before that have become characteristic of the person.

If syndromes are comprised of needs, it may seem as if there would be but few types, there being only physiological, safety, belongingness and love, esteem, self-actualization, and cognitive understanding needs. According to Maslow, however, each of those categories are conglomerates of related needs, rather than only one need and, even more important, although the needs on the hierarchy are universal for the species, they achieve myriad expressions among the members of the species. In all this, there is potential enough for theoretical understanding of diversity and individuality. The word "potential" is used advisedly, however, for Maslow hardly scratched the surface of the task of providing a specific, detailed statement about the varieties of need expression.

Although Maslow did not actually provide a list of syndromes or types, it is clear that, if he had done so, the basis for the list would be the assumption that persons progress up the hierarchy of needs only so far as the available gratifications permit.

> If most people have similar emotional needs, each person can be compared with any other in the degree to which these needs are satisifed. This is a holistic or organismic principle because it classifies whole persons on a single continuum rather than parts or aspects or persons on a multiplicity of unrelated continua. (Maslow, 1954, p. 117)

The single continuum referred to in this quote is, of course, the hierarchy of needs. So, although Maslow did not really go much further in his thinking, we may presume that a list of complexes would include a physiological type, a safety type, a belongingness and love type, an esteem type, a self-actualization type and a cognitive understanding type, these types corresponding roughly to the amount of development permitted by the person's life experiences. Indeed, Maslow discusses what a self-actualization type would be like. His thinking about this will be reviewed later.

Although Maslow does not offer a complete list of types, he details some general properties pertaining to all types, regardless of their content (Maslow, 1954, pp. 37–61). The first characteristic of types or syndromes is *interchangeability,* the quality whereby all parts of a syndrome are equivalent in having the same aim, and can therefore substitute for each other, and have equal probability of appearance. In a secure person, for example, all behavioral expressions are interchangeable in the sense that they all express security. Another

type characteristic is *circular determination,* which refers to
"the continual flux of dynamic interaction within a syndrome,
whereby any one part is always affected by all other parts,
the entire action going on simultaneously" (ibid.). Yet another characteristic is *the tendency of well-organized syndromes to resist change,* by which Maslow emphasizes the
essential irreversability of something so pervasive as a life
style, which organizes and integrates diverse aspects of functioning toward one overall end. Closely related to this characteristic is one referring to *the. tendency of a syndrome to re-
establish itself after change.* What Maslow means is that,
while syndromes do not spontaneously change, if change is
forced by environmental pressure the syndrome will tend to
reappear essentially unchanged once the pressure eases. Another characteristic referring to change states that *syndromes
tend to change as a whole.* Although it is hardly clear from
Maslow's writing what constitutes the conditions under which
syndromes do change, it is presumed that he meant here to
suggest that, if environmental pressure toward change continues long enough or is intense enough, the syndrome will
finally change, rather than merely be suppressed. But when
change occurs, however, it will tend to take place in the syndrome as a whole rather than in one or another element of
the syndrome. An implication of this is that change will be
rapid when and if it does occur. Another characteristic that
seems to overlap with some already mentioned is that syndromes tend to be internally consistent, by which Maslow
means to invoke the Gestalt principle of "good-form." To
Maslow, " . . . a person who is insecure tends to become more
perfectly or consistently insecure; a person who is high in self-
esteem tends to become more consistently high in self-esteem."
(Maslow, 1954, p. 43). Maslow lists a few other characteristics, but these are too close in meaning to those already
mentioned to be anything but redundant.

Maslow's approach toward characteristic types is promising, as far as it has been developed. But it has not been developed far enough to actually permit its use in such endeavors as the diagnosis of the type of personality a person possesses. One has the feeling that if and when such development is attempted a whole raft of vexing problems will be uncovered. Now perhaps this is the kind of thing that makes personology interesting.

Before leaving this discussion, it should be noted that Murray (1938) also theorizes in terms of complexes. His typology, which is heavily dependent on the views of Freud, includes the well-known *oral, anal, castration* (or phallic) *complexes,* and adds emphasis to the *claustral* and *urethral complexes* as well. As in psychoanalytic theory, complexes are produced by developmental arrests or *fixations,* according to Murray. These matters will be discussed further in Chapter four. What is important for now is to appreciate something of the content that has been specified for these complexes. In the adult, the various possible claustral complexes all represent residuals of the uterine or prenatal experience. These complexes can be of three types:

> (1) a complex constellated about the wish to reinstate the conditions similar to those prevailing before birth, (2) a complex that centers about the anxiety of insupport and helplessness, and (3) a complex that is anxiously directed against suffocation and confinement. (Murray, 1938, p. 363)

Oral complexes can be of a succorant variety, in which passivity and dependence are uppermost; or an aggressive variety, characterized by ambivalence toward authority, phobias, and stuttering; of rejection, including diarrhea, disorder, and autonomy; or of retention, involving order, cleanliness, possessiveness, and autonomy. Murray does not detail the castration complexes, but agrees with Freud that they stem from anxiety and guilt concerning sexual use of the genitalia.

Among psychoanalysts, Murray is unusual in the amount

of emphasis he puts on the urethral complexes. In his early writings, Murray (1938) tended to include here bed-wetting and urethral erotism, with little further elaboration. More recently, Murray (1955) has given special importance to urethral fixations in understanding the competitiveness and ambition so rampant in our society. He has named one form of urethral fixation the *Icarus complex,* after the mythological personage who flew too near to the sun in his attempt to surpass his father, and as a result had the wax holding his artificial wings melt, leaving him unable to fly. People with the Icarus complex are considered to have a special affinity for fire and water, strong narcissism, cravings for immortality, and great aspirations that crumble in the face of failure.

Interrelationships Between the More and Less General Concepts

When one turns to a consideration of the relationship between very general concepts and the relatively concrete ones that refer more directly to regularities of functioning, Allport and Murray leave unfortunate ambiguities. In Murray's position, there is no definite superordinate establishment that is to subsume the numerous needs that develop through learning and the accrual of experience. These needs are certainly not innate, and therefore not part of the id. They are probably not considered components of the superego or ego ideal because these are constituted primarily of values, taboos, and standards for evaluation. But the ego ideal, at least, has motivational properties, that is, aspirations, and leads to the formation of serial programs (Murray and Kluckhohn, 1956, pp. 26–28). To complicate things further, the recent value-vector version of the need makes clear what was already less explicitly included in such earlier concepts as the need-integrate, namely, that needs include values. If the ego contains only generic abilities, then even though it develops largely through interaction with the environment it would not seem to subsume the more specific need concept. But Murray's most extensive description of the ego does not permit one to be certain that he definitely means to exclude the specific, learned, habitual styles of coping from the company of the more general, pervasive abilities (Murray and Kluckhohn, 1956, pp. 24–26). Perhaps he does not wish to keep the two kinds of units separate. This would explain Murray's tentative suggestion that general systems of learned needs may constitute the ego (ibid., p. 31).

Needless to say, it would be useful to have further clarification of the relationship between learned needs on the one hand and the id, super-ego, ego, and ego-ideal on the other. A reasonable lead, which does not seem inconsistent with Murray's general intent, would be to consider learned needs (value-vectors), need-integrates, and perhaps thema to be personality units that are formed out of the interaction between the establishments (reasonably well formed before adulthood is reached, and representing the general influence of society, innate needs, developing generic capacities) and the specific environmental encounters that occur during living. The learned needs would then exist as a more changeable, less central, though more immediately expressed layer of personality. In such a scheme, it would be more possible to give the various subcharacteristics of the establishments a clear causal role in the development of learned needs.

In a recent discussion (Allport, 1961, pp, 100–38), but not in his earlier statement (Allport, 1955, pp. 41–56), Allport also leaves one uncertain as to whether it is only general, pervasive functions or functions plus specific classes of personal dispositions that are to comprise the proprium. If the proprium is meant to be a collection of interdependent and important personal dispositions, then the propriate functions could not logically play a causal role in the formation of these dispositions. A possibly useful lead, similar to that suggested above, would be to consider that the propriate functions are not themselves combinations of dispositions, but rather the major forces precipitating and combining with the individual's life experiences to form the simpler units. For example, propriate striving would refer to the propensity in an individual for phenomenally important intentioning, because of which it would be possible to develop cardinal and central dispositions having dynamic properties.

Allport may be moving to show propriate functions as major forces in his attempt to conceptualize components of personality that seem to be sets of personal dispositions which reflect the qualities of propriate functioning. Examples of this type of unit are Allport's characteristics of maturity, such as specific, enduring extensions of the self, techniques for relating warmly to others (such as tolerance), stable emotional security or self-acceptance, habits of realistic perception, skills and problem-centeredness, established self-objectification in the form of insight and humor, and a unifying philosophy of life including particular value orientations, differentiated religious sentiment, and a generic personalized conscience (Allport, 1961, pp. 275–307).

If one were to focus upon the high level of abilities consistent with Murray's idea of the strong ego (Murray and Kluckhohn, 1956, pp. 24–26), and consider the specific learned methods of styles by which these abilities are expressed by individuals, one would arrive at characteristics similar in many respects to Allport's criteria of maturity. Some of Allport's other stated characteristics come closer to the aspects of personality subsumed by Murray under the concepts of ego-ideal and superego. In these, Allport, even more than Murray, presents a view of conscience and aspirations that departs from the original Freudian view by being personal, highly differentiated, and the project of considerable assimilated adult experience, rather than a simple carry-over of the relatively unchanged cultural values and taboos that were implanted at a psychologically tender age.

Maslow was more explicit than Allport and Murray (though hardly complete) in discussing the nature of the interrelationship between more and less general concepts. As indicated before, syndromes are clearly composed of need expressions. And need expressions reflect the level in the need hierarchy at which the person is functioning. Although Maslow did not really go very far in filling out the content implications of these relational statements, it must be said that he presents a fairly clear picture of the outlines of a position on personality that integrates the general and the specific concepts. Many questions remain to be answered, however, even if one avoids considerations of content *per se*. Does a syndrome include only the need expressions characteristic of the set of needs expressive of the person's place on the hierarchy, or does it include expressions of needs at levels below that as well? Although one would presume the latter, from Maslow's (1954, p. 102) emphasis on behavior as multi-determined, it is hard to be sure. Recognizing that for each set of needs on the hierarchy there are many possible expressions, is there any way to understand the circumstances under which some expressions rather than others will be present in a particular syndrome?

4

Development of Ideal and Nonideal Personalities

A brief consideration of personality development will provide yet another vantage point from which to observe the inter-relationship of concepts and the influence of assumptions about the nature of man.

Allport believes that the infant has little personality, his undifferentiated, opportunistic behavior being determined by ongoing biochemical processes and environmental pressures (Allport, 1961, pp. 57–307). Initially, the infant can only express discomfort in relatively reflexive ways when strong viscerogenic needs exist. He functions according to the principle of tension reduction alone. During this early period, the infant is extremely dependent upon others, particularly his mother, for succorance and affection. If these are readily obtained, then the preconditions for the development of a gradually more differentiated and personally integrated life style or personality are met.

With enough security, the kernels of selfhood begin to develop near the end of the first year of life, Allport states. The first signs of consciousness take the form of recogniz-able experience of the body (bodily sense). The second and third years see the beginnings of self-identity and then self-esteem. From four to six, the child develops some self-extension and self-image, and from six to twelve, the rational coping qualities of the proprium become apparent. In adolescence, propriate striving is in increasing evidence. Although these various propriate functions begin their development at different ages, they are all interdependent, and become unified even further with the gradual development of the knowing function.

As the proprium expands and grows in strength in adolescence, an ever widening system of personal dispositions is formed, Allport states. All the while, opportunistic functioning concerned with reducing tension caused by survival needs recedes in importance and is replaced by propriate functioning and striving, which involves increases in or maintenance of tension. Propriate functioning is a reflection of the tendency toward psychological growth that is part of the nature of man. Development continues on into adulthood, which is normally marked by the emergence of signs of maturity.

If an infant's early dependency is not warmly met, Allport continues, the child may later react with signs of insecurity, initially including aggression and demandingness, and later including jealousy and egoism. Vigorous development of propriate functioning will be jeopardized, and the individual will remain relatively undifferentiated and deficient in consciously controlled living. Tension reduction will remain an important aim. Such an individual would be considered mentally ill.

Murray's view of development is an elaboration and extension of that view associated with psychoanalytic tradition (Murray, 1938, pp. 282–396; Murray and Kluckhohn, 1956, pp. 41–49). Initially, the infant does possess some personality in the form of acceptable and unacceptable id impulses. With more experience and socialization he begins to develop an ego, and then a superego and ego-ideal. Murray divides early life into five stages of development, claustral (intrauterine), oral, anal, urethral, and phallic. Each stage is characterized by highly enjoyable conditions, inevitably brought to an end by socializing forces from the external environment. If the external forces overfrustrate or underfrustrate the child, a fixation will occur. This arresting of psychological growth, if it is severe or occurs frequently, will leave its mark on the developing personality in the form of a *complex* (Murray, 1938, pp. 361–93). An apparently related concept is the *unity-thema* (ibid., pp. 604–605), a combination of need-press units functioning as a relatively unconscious, dynamic component of personality which, though formed in early life, continues to exert considerable influence upon later functioning.

If complexes affecting a developing personality are not too many or too strong, the personality will continue to show considerable change on into adulthood, Murray says. The individual will gradually accrue a strong ego that adds flexibility, consciousness, and effectiveness to functioning, a personalized, sophisticated superego, a realistic ego-ideal, and many interrelated, learned needs. All this will occur because of the growth potential, reflected in the constructive id impulses and the innate ego potential, and because of the necessity of reducing conflicts produced by the unsocialized id impulses in interaction with the external world. The general aim of functioning will not be to maintain a low level of tension, but rather to experience the pleasurable process of tension reduction. As the individual grows in experience, he will learn to permit and encourage the build-up of tension so that the ensuing pleasure at its dissipation can be increased.

Recently Murray has suggested the value of distinguishing three periods of life: the first era, "marked by the emergence and multiplication of potentialities for a high proportion of new, develpmental . . . structural components, each with its consequential psychological properties"; the second era (middle age) "marked by a relatively high proportion of conservative recompositions of the already developed structures and functions"; and the third era (senescence), which "is marked by a decrease of potentialities for new compositions and recompositions. . . ." (Murray, 1968, pp. 8–10) Although one can readily agree with such distinctions, it is too early in their formulation to gain any clear picture of the use to which Murray will put them in his theory of personality. In all likelihood, however, this recent formulation indicates an even further distancing from traditional Freudian beliefs, though Murray certainly means to retain some emphasis on the metabolic, somatic capabilities of the organism as one defining feature of the developmental process. In this recent statement, the other defining feature of development is the hedonic calculus of pleasures and pains. Here Murray apparently subscribes to the belief that a person avoids pain and pursues pleasure. This position seems to be slightly at variance with his earlier statement concerning the willful building up of tension in order to increase the intensity of pleasure when tension is finally discharged.

Murray considers human personality to be to a large degree a compromise between the individual's own impulses and the demands and interests of other people (Murray and Kluckhohn, 1956, pp. 45–48). Normality is a state of optimal compromise, where needs can be expressed in socialized fashion, and consciousness is present. Mental illness is associated with either undersocialization or oversocialization.

Maslow's views on development have already been alluded to in previous discussions. The hierarchy of needs is considered to be a developmental continuum, starting with the physiological needs and progressing to the need for self-actualization. Although Maslow (1964a) hardly elaborates the aspects of the environment considered beneficial or deleterious by his conceptualization of the hierarchy of needs, it seems rather apparent that the person must receive sufficient gratifications from the environment in order for each rung on the ladder to be climbed. Thus, nutrients and other survival necessities must be available if the person is to progress from the level of physiological needs; a minimization of danger is required for progression beyond safety needs; social rootedness and nurturance are necessary to progress from needs for belongingness and love; and acceptance and respect are necessary for the progression beyond esteem needs to take place. Thus far one can anticipate the developmental implications of Maslow's position. It is worth noting that even though the principle of tension reduction governs functioning at these lower need levels, the satisfaction of a need does not imply satiation and quiescence. The easing of tension must be intended as very temporary.

> . . . gratification of one need and its consequent removal from the center of the stage brings about not a state of rest, but rather the emergence into consciousness of another higher need. (Maslow, 1955)

Turning now to the higher needs, which will emerge as the lower needs are satisfied, we find it difficult to imagine the environmental circumstances, if any, that satisfy the needs for self-actualization and cognitive understanding in Maslow's thinking. These two needs are probably not to be considered dependent on environmental circumstances. Maslow seems to have meant that if the lower needs are met then the natural propensity for expressing or actualizing one's inherent potentialities and concern with understanding self and world can proceed vigorously. This means that the higher needs cannot be satisfied by external events, but require instead that the organism express itself (Maslow, 1955). In such expression, tension increase takes place (due to increases in growth and differentiation) and is not experienced as obnoxious. Indeed, tension increase may actually be part of the satisfaction of development (Maslow, 1961, 1965).

As can be seen, Maslow's position is quite similar in form, and fairly similar in content, to that of Allport. Although

Maslow is unclear about when during one's lifetime satisfaction of the various sets of needs must occur if development up the hierarchy of needs is not to be jeopardized, the emphasis on self-actualization and cognitive understanding as ideals of maturity suggests that development certainly does not stop with the passing of childhood. Whether or not the lower survival needs must be satisfied early in life in order for the higher needs to achieve full expression, the very nature of that full expression bespeaks a lifelong process of realizing the richness of one's potentialities. Like Allport, Maslow believed that this growth process occurs spontaneously, as long as the survival needs have been met. If there is any motivational principle or triggering force toward growth, it is the boredom that plagues a healthy organism once it has achieved mastery of some possibility, so that it falls to a routine level.

> Growth takes place when the next step forward is subjectively more delightful, more joyous, more intrinsically satisfying than the last. The only way we can ever know what is right for us is that it feels better subjectively than any alternative. (Maslow, 1956, p. 36)

This curiosity, or exploratory tendency, is the rudimentary expression of the needs for self-actualization and cognitive understanding, and this expression will not take place unless lower needs have been met.

> The child who is fortunate enough to grow normally and well gets satiated and bored with the delights that he has savored and sufficiently and eagerly (without pushing) goes on to higher, more complex delights as they become available to him without danger or threat. (Maslow, 1956, p. 45)

This quote clearly states that the higher needs cannot be satisfied, but can only be inhibited, by environmental events.

Finally, it should be mentioned that Maslow (1955) detailed the content of one syndrome of personality, that which

results when a person has successfully transcended the survival needs and is leading a life expressive of self-actualization and cognitive understanding. The common features, or
traits, of this mature personality type are (1) *realistic orientation,* or the ability to see self and world accurately, (2)
acceptance of self, others, and the natural world, (3) *spontaneity,* or the ability to experience and impliment one's reactions straightforwardly, (4) *task orientation,* rather than
self-preoccupation, (5) *sense of privacy,* (6) *independence,*
(7) vivid *appreciativeness,* (8) *spirituality* that is not necessarily religious in a formal sense, (9) sense of *identity with
mankind,* (10) feelings of intimacy with a few loved ones,
(11) *democratic values,* (12) recognition of the *difference
between means and ends,* (13) *humor* that is philosophical
rather than hostile, (14) *creativeness,* and (15) *nonconformism.* Although this list is long and heterogeneous enough to
escape easy integration into an organized picture of personality, it is certainly consistent with Maslow's general emphasis
on a rational, principled, integrated approach to life as the
mark of mental health. This personality syndrome bears striking resemblance to Allport's criteria of maturity. In attempting to be a bit more concrete about this personality type,
Maslow suggests that it was possessed by certain notable
persons, including Lincoln, Jefferson, Jane Addams, William
James, Eleanor Roosevelt, and Einstein.

The similarities among the accounts of development made
by Allport, Maslow, and Murray include great emphasis upon
an active, influential consciousness, the assumption (however vaguely formulated) of an inherent growth tendency, a
view of development as continuing into adulthood with related
emphasis upon the complex differentiations and integrations
of maturity, and a belief that personality is largely learned.

Our theorists also differ. One difference is a disparity in emphasis upon individual differences. This difference is reflected
in Murray's assumption that a common portion of personality

is present at birth, and in his stress on the degree to which the personality is fashioned through conflict with socializing forces, even to the point of using that degree of socialization as an index of psychological health. These ideas imply that men are fairly similar to one another. In some ways, Maslow's emphasis is similar. He assumes that the hierarchy of needs is species wide, and since it is these needs that heavily condition the type of personality that people may develop, there is clear emphasis upon common features of mankind. But—more than Murray—Maslow concerns himself with the myriad ways in which the species-wide needs may find expression in particular people. Maslow seems to fall somewhere between Murray and Allport in emphasis on uniqueness.

Allport, the most extreme proponent of individuality, finds no inherited personality components common to all, and limits the role of social forces to that of providing or failing to provide the necessary background conditions for adequate personality development. Not only does Allport's conceptualization of health and illness have little to do with socialization, but one suspects that a fair degree of social autonomy would be necessary in his view of maturity. Development is somewhat more continuous for Murray than for Allport, the latter stressing the radical difference in existence precipitated by the appearance of the proprium. Allport also details development during adulthood to a greater degree than does Murray, although both believe that such development is important.

Despite the great importance Maslow, Allport, and Murray all give to learning, none has provided a satisfactory account of the specific processes and mechanisms involved. Murray simply assumes learning, and appears to subscribe to general principles of reinforcement. He also believes that learned needs are developed in some way out of unlearned ones (Murray, 1938, pp. 76–77, 80). But this is not to say that learned needs are considered so transistory that they will extinguish rapidly unless occasionally revitalized by direct association with unlearned needs. Murray goes no further. And this is actually further than Maslow went. It is not even clear whether Maslow subscribed to orthodox principles of reinforcement, such as contiguity of stimulus and response, and tension reduction as a basis for learning.

Allport, who like Murray believed that learned dispositions are quite independent of the dispositions that may have led to their formation, introduced the descriptive term of *functional autonomy* to refer "to any acquired system of motivation in which the tensions involved are not of the same kind as the antecedent tensions from which the acquired system developed." (Allport, 1961, p. 229). In attempting to add clarification, Allport distinguished perseverative and propriate functional autonomy, the former being less central, more the stuff of habits, than is the latter. The possible mechanisms suggested whereby the perseverative type may come about seem to function either through some physiological reverberatory mechanism that becomes fairly stable or by the appetitive influence of novelty associated with the learning situation (ibid., pp. 244–49). Propriate functional autonomy comes about because the presumed energy potential possessed by the human is in excess of that contributed by survival needs, and hence there is an ongoing tendency to utilize this excess by increasing competence and pressing toward a unification of life (ibid., pp. 249–53). Allport's thinking remains somewhat vague concerning specific mechanisms whereby functional autonomy takes place, and thus provides a number of bases for controversy. He does not circumvent the repeated criticism that functional autonomy is more of an assertion than an explanation, although he suggested that an extremely critical reception indicates an already closed mind when he wrote that his concept "is merely a way of stating that men's motives change and grow in the course of life, because it is the nature of man that they should do so. Only theorists wedded to a reactive, homeostatic, quasi-closed model of man find difficulty in agreeing" (ibid., pp. 252–53).

5

Representative Research

Over the years, Allport, Maslow, and Murray have each done many diverse pieces of research. Despite the wide range of topics considered, there is a striking consistency in the approaches of these theorists both singly and together. It is not feasible to review all of the research they have done, and, happily, it is not necessary to be so comprehensive in order to discover their general approach. What you will find here is a summary of some of the more important and representative studies done by each theorist, along with an explication of the humanistic themes running through the work. In addition, we will sketch some of the most direct influences these men have had on the research of others.

Allport's Research

Perhaps the most characteristic of Allport's research enterprises was his study of expressive movement. You will recall that he theorized about the difference between dynamic and expressive traits, considering the former to entail motivated, coping behavior, and the latter to entail stylistic, habitual behavior. Stemming from this distinction between traits was a pioneering study by Allport and Vernon (1933) in which the actions of 25 subjects were scrutinized to determine whether

there was sufficient consistency in their expressive movements
to justify the belief in the importance of expressive traits. The
25 subjects were tested three times, each test four weeks apart.
During each testing session, the subjects responded to a large
number of different tests providing measures of speed of reading and counting; speed of walking and strolling; length of
stride; estimation of familiar sizes and distances; estimation of
weights; strength of handshake; speed and pressure of finger,
hand, and leg tapping; drawing squares, circles, and other
figures; various handwriting measures; muscular tension; and
so forth. In addition, observer ratings were obtained for various measures, such as voice intensity, speech fluency, and neatness of appearance.

The first question asked by Allport and Vernon about the
subjects' actions was whether these various expressive measures
showed sufficient stability over the three testing sessions to
demonstrate that continuing aspects of personality were being
studied. In general, the estimates of stability were reasonably
high and compared favorably to stability for self-descriptive
(questionnaire) measures of personality. Allport and Vernon
then studied the relationship between scores for the same tasks
performed by different muscle groups, such as left and right
sides of the body, and arms and legs. In striking results, they
found about the same level of consistency as had been reported
for the same muscle groups over a period of time. Perhaps there
is some general or central integrating factor that produces a
consistent style no matter what peripheral mechanisms are observed.

The final analysis attempted in Allport and Vernon's study
was the intercorrelation of 38 of the major variables from all
the tasks. A form of cluster analysis roughly comparable to
factor analysis was employed. Three factors emerged. The first,
or *areal factor,* included such variables as area of total writing,
area of blackboard figures, and length of self-rating checks.
The important trait involved here seems to be motor expan-

siveness. The second factor seems to involve *extroversion-introversion,* including such measures as overestimation of distance from the body, and underestimation of weights. The third factor, called *factor of emphasis,* includes such measures as voice intensity, movement during speech, writing pressure, and tapping pressure.

In an attempt to further document the contention that expressive movement can be valuable in diagnosing the personality, Allport and Vernon followed the analyses mentioned above with four case histories in which the subject's expressive movements were compared to known characteristics of their personalities. Allport and Vernon conclude that "virtually no measurements contradict the subjective impression of the personalities. The measures faithfully record what common sense dictates" (Allport and Vernon, 1933, p. 180). In addition, judges were able to match handwriting samples and kymographic curves (indicating pressure exerted while writing) with personality sketches in a better than chance manner. Since Allport and Vernon's pioneering study, several other studies done by Allport's students have tended to confirm the finding that personality ratings can be sucessfully matched with various indices of expressive movement.

In another study (Allport and Cantril, 1934) it was shown that judges could estimate personality accurately on the basis of voice cues alone. More than 600 judges were employed to judge 16 speakers. Various kinds of ratings of personality and expressive movements were made by the judges solely on the basis of the voice quality of the speakers. At a level exceeding chance, the judges successfully predicted both physical characteristics and personality traits from voice cues, although they were better at the latter. That they were better at predicting personality traits suggests that expressive characteristics are to be understood more as aspects of personality than mere physical manifestations.

In a very different kind of research, Allport and Vernon

(1933) devised a test of values that continues to be quite important today. They began with Spranger's six value areas—namely, economic, theoretical, aesthetic, social, political, and religious—and proceeded to devise questionnaire items reflecting a commitment to these areas. The criterion for final item selection was internal consistency within each of the six areas. In the more contemporary version of the test, called the *Study of Values* (Allport, Vernon, and Lindzey, 1951), a fair amount of information concerning reliability and validity has been accumulated.

Allport, Vernon, and Lindzey's scales show adequate reliability and very little intercorrelation. Separate norms on the various scales have been provided for men and women, based on a college population. Most of the validity information takes the form of demonstrating that various educational and occupational groups show the value profiles that one might expect. For example, medical students showed theoretical values as their highest area, whereas the religious area was highest for theological students. Some relationship has also been shown between value profiles and academic achievement, and between this test of values and others. The *Study of Values* has achieved wide popularity as one of the few available ways of assessing values. Regardless of the incomplete nature of validation, few psychologists dispute that people with different value profiles will behave differently.

Murray's Research

Murray's (1938) major contribution to personality research was a pioneering study that was truly grand in scope. He and a capable staff of personologists collected huge amounts of data relating to his list of needs (for example, achievement, affiliation, nurturance) on a group of 50 college males. Over a period of six months or so, the subjects were scrutinized through all sorts of measurement—questionnaires, fantasy tests, and behavior ratings—to gain a comprehensive picture of personality.

Being unwilling to overlook any possibly relevant observation that someone might make, Murray instituted the diagnostic council as an alternative to fixed tests objectively scored. In this council debate would ensue as to what was actually being observed in a subject. A conclusion would then be reached by majority vote. Most psychologists would today regard this as very unscientific practice, but it should be remembered that personality research was then in its infancy and that Murray regarded his work as mainly exploratory. Even if the findings cannot be taken as demonstrating the empirical existence and validity of some of the concepts in Murray's theory, the study was a brave beginning. The research report is rich with insights into the personalities of the subjects, and bears an amount of information not frequently matched in the understanding of personality.

A gauge of the influence of Murray's pioneering study is that some of its measuring devices are still in active use today. Notable among these devices is the Thematic Apperception Test (Morgan and Murray, 1935), which, next to the Rorschach Test, is the one most relied upon by clinicians. Murray has always been ingenious in devising measuring instruments well suited to the problem being studied.

Subsequent to the study just described, Murray and Morgan (1945) conducted an investigation of sentiments that utilized a similar approach in terms of comprehensiveness and richness of data. Other early studies made by Murray include an examination of the contention that dreams are clairvoyant (Murray and Wheeler, 1936), which capitalized on a naturally occuring tragedy and peoples' dreams concerning it, and a clinical interpretation of the psychological meaning of Melville's novel, *Moby Dick* (Murray, 1951b).

A recent investigation reported by Murray shows many of the same methodological emphases of his earlier work (Murray, 1963). The general aim of this study was to determine the effects of participating in stressful interpersonal disputations. Twenty-five college males were studied intensively over

a period of months by a group of personologists. The subjects
were (1) given a month to write an essay on their personal
philosophies of life, (2) made to debate the pros and cons of
their position with an accomplice described as a talented young
lawyer, (3) informed that a moving picture would be made
of the debate, and (4) subjected to a procedure for recording
heart and respiration rate during the debate. The debate took
place in three six-minute periods. By prearrangement, the accomplice became increasingly more vehement and hostile over
the three periods. After the debate, the subjects were (1)
asked to write down everything they remembered about it, (2)
encouraged to relax and relive the debate in the context of a
supportive interviewer, and (3) required to answer a series
of specific questions concerning emotional reactions to the debate. In an extraordinary attempt to be comprehensive, the
design called for subjects to return no less than four times
subsequent to the debate in order to discuss various remem-
brances of it, and finally, to view the film of it and discuss the
reactions thus provoked.

At the time of the report being discussed, not all of the rich
sources of information provided by it had been analysed. The
report focuses upon angry reactions to the stressful debate. In
characteristic fashion, anger is richly defined as having overt
manifestations (for example, verbal productions clearly intended to express anger, vocal qualities such as louder and
more rapid speech), covert manifestations (for example, agres-
sive words or voice qualities that seem to intrude on an otherwise cool interaction, reports of felt anger not communicated
otherwise), and psyiological manifestations (for example, au-
tonomic excitations, increases in respiration rate). The report
deals primarily with the physiological manifestations, and
makes some interesting points. In general, the average heart
rate of subjects (1) is high in anticipation of the debate, (2)
drops during the first, relatively unstressful part of the debate,
and (3) increases as the accomplice becomes more abusive.

But group and individual differences abound. One group of subjects rated as having high drive shows the same shape of curve as do low-drive subjects, but with generally higher average levels. As to individual differences, several subjects showed curves deviating from the shape of the average curve, with at least one subject's heart rate actually declining as the accomplice became more abusive. Further analyses of the data available in this study will attempt to correlate the heart rate results with the more phenomenological information.

Maslow's Research

One of Maslow's best known studies was aimed at determining the personality characteristics of great, creative people, past and present. The people included Lincoln, Jefferson, Eleanor Roosevelt, Walt Whitman, Thoreau, Beethoven, and Einstein. To this notable company, Maslow added several of his own friends and other contemporary persons noted by their peers as being extraordinary. The data scrutinized and interpretative procedures utilized are not very well described by Maslow, but it is clear that he took the same kind of approach that the clinician takes and that was taken by Murray in his study of *Moby Dick*. In other words, one scrutinizes whatever documents are available, interviews where that is possible, and tries to look for threads of similarity within each case and across several cases. These threads of similarity are the personality characteristics being sought. Just what Maslow found, constituting his statement on the mature or self-actualizing personality has already been covered in Chapter three. You will recall that the relevant characteristics of a mature personality include such things as spontaneity, nonconformism, and democratic values. Strictly speaking, this study cannot be considered confirmation of Maslow's theorizing, because the scrutiny of data constituted the basis upon which the conceptualization was formulated. This is the same situation we encountered in Murray's (1938) study of needs.

A study by Maslow and Mintz (1956) investigates the possibility that one's surroundings affect one's judgments. Subjects were asked to judge the amount of "energy" and "sense of well-being" in the faces shown in a series of photographs. Some of the subjects made their judgments while in a beautifully appointed room, other subjects while in a dirty, ugly room, and still other subjects in an average room. Sex of experimenter and order of picture presentation were varied so as to insure no biasing effect from these quarters. The results indicate clearly that subjects making their judgments in a beautiful room saw more energy and well-being in the faces that did subjects in either the average or ugly rooms. But subjects judging in the ugly room did not perform differently from subjects in the average room. So, we can conclude that the beauty of one's surroundings disposes one to be generous and optimistic.

In a study exploring the relationship of personal security to the judgments one makes, Maslow (1957) found that secure subjects judge photographs of faces to be more warm than do subjects who are insecure. Security and insecurity were measured by a questionnaire of Maslow's construction. Using the same questionnaire to separate secure and insecure groups, Maslow and Szilagyi-Kessler (1946) found that the secure subjects had either never been breast fed or were breast fed for more than one year, whereas the insecure subjects tended to have been breast fed for less than one year. The study offers a complex interpretation of these findings.

Earlier in his career, Maslow (1939, 1942) did research on the importance of self-esteem (or dominance feelings, as he suggests it should be called) in the lives of women. As a graduate student, Maslow (1936) had observed that sexuality in primates can be well understood as expressive of dominance relationships. Whatever might be called a sex drive seemed less important than the dominance relationship. These studies of lower animals served as a stimulus to Maslow's work with human females. One has the feeling that, later in life, Maslow would not have been as interested in generalizing from primate to man. But in those early days he was still deeply influenced by Harry Helson and his other graduate-school mentors.

Maslow (1942) reasoned that the human situation bears a definite resemblance to the primate level, though much more complex. In an attempt to demonstrate this, he interviewed and gave questionnaires to upwards of 100 women. He thus was able to measure their *dominance feelings* (self-esteem), actual *dominance status* (social position), *dominance behavior* (domineering actions), various facets of *sexual behavior* (for example, masturbation, frequency of intercourse), and *sexual drive* (roughly defined physiological need for sex). Maslow was the first to admit the rough, even overlapping, nature of the measurements, though there were sufficiently extensive and different sources of information to provoke some confidence in his procedures. The interviews were quite open-ended, with the justification that the attempt to understand each subject in her own terms was more important than the slavish repetition of questions from subject to subject.

Consistent with expectation, Maslow's study found that sex drive and dominance feeling have little or no correlation, and that it is the latter rather than the former that shows the highest relationships to such signs of sexual behavior as promiscuity, masturbation, and sexual attitude. Masturbation and non-virginity were found to go together, suggesting that masturbation should not be thought of as only a method of compensating for the absence of heterosexual experience. Even homosexuality seemed to be more a function of dominance feelings than sex drive. The women having such homosexual experiences described the experiences as a means of gaining power over other women. The best marriages emerged as those in which both partners were of about equal dominance feeling. In Maslow's sample, divorced women had higher dominance feeling scores than married women. This is consistent with the finding that

marriages tend to be poor when women are higher in dominance feeling than their husbands.

In characterizing the difference between primate and human
sexuality, Maslow stresses that the dominance *status* determines sexual behavior in the primate, whereas in the human
the dominance *feeling* determines such behavior. Thus human sexuality is much more controlled by personality than is
the case in primates. Although the correlation between dominance status and dominance feeling in humans is moderate,
it is clear that dominance feeling is contributed to by many
factors in experience beyond the sheer fact of the status one
enjoys.

One striking theme in the research of Allport, Maslow, and
Murray is that a lot of information is obtained about each subject participating in the study. Murray (1938), for example,
used numerous questionnaires, interviews, fantasy tests, performance tasks, and behavioral ratings in attempting a description of the motivations of his subjects. Similarly, Allport and
Vernon (1933) engaged in repeated observations of the actions and verbal behavior of their subjects, and Maslow (1955)
scrutinized many records and observed behavior wherever possible. A central emphasis of humanistically oriented research
is to describe the entire personality—not only all its parts, but
also the holistic flavor of the integration of these parts. Therefore, extensive data collection is deemed necessary even if the
effort and expense entailed results in decreasing the number of
subjects studied to below that which is customary. By implication, Allport, Maslow, and Murray all believe that, if the description of personality is complete enough, there will be little
risk of reaching inaccurate conclusions about man in general,
even if the number of subjects studied has been quite small.

Allport, Maslow, and Murray all tend to collect their observations of subjects over a number of testing sessions, with
the time span involved being sufficient to insure that what is
being observed is a truly consistent phenomenon. In general,

humanistically inspired research has little use for one-shot data collection. Instead such research emphasizes multiple testing sessions and the establishment of surprisingly close relationships between experimenters and subjects. It should be remembered that Murray (1938, 1963) commonly came to know his subjects quite well, that Allport and Vernon (1933) employed several testing sessions, and that Maslow (1955) even used some of his friends as subjects.

Another characteristic feature of the research of these three theorists is the emphasis upon subjects who are at least normal or average, and frequently extraordinary in education, talent, and intelligence. Allport and Vernon (1933) and Murray (1938) used articulate, intelligent, well-educated college students, and Maslow (1955) focused upon great men. This is in sharp contrast to the frequent tendency to use psychopathological persons in case study and laboratory research. The three theorists have chosen to study extraordinary persons because, in this fashion, they can better understand man's potentialities and the process of actualizing them. You will recall that this optimistic, future-oriented emphasis upon what is fine in life is a hallmark of the humanistic stance. In their choice of research subjects, Allport, Maslow, and Murray are challenging the orthodox contention of clinical psychologists and psychiatrists that, in the study of psychopathology, one can come to understand mental health.

The general emphasis upon complete data collection and establishment of close relationships between experimenter and subject brings us to another feature of the research we have been considering. It is common for Allport, Maslow, and Murray to so plan their data collection procedures that the natural behaviors of their subjects are distorted as little as possible. The theorists tend not to perform experiments in the usual sense, which manipulates the subjects in some way and then observes the effects of such manipulation. Rather, Allport, Maslow, and Murray observe their subjects in performance situations that give the subjects a wide latitude for action. They employ open-ended interviews in nontaxing circumstances, and use ambiguous test stimuli for the subject to shape in his own way. In addition, already existing documents by or about the subject are scrutinized. In all this, we see the humanist's conviction that the task of understanding the person is best pursued through naturalistic observation with a minimum of manipulation. This conviction flies in the face of current orthodoxy, in which the gauge of research acceptability is the degree to which the study approaches the experimental control common in physics. In defending themselves, Allport, Maslow, and Murray point to the naturalistic, correlational research of such shapers of modern belief as Darwin, Freud, and the host of astronomers who cannot perform meaningful experiments at all.

Finally, we should mention a word about the methodological ingenuity of Allport, Maslow, and Murray. It may seem peculiar to consider their research as showing methodological ingenuity, because their experimental designs and treatments of data are frequently quite rudimentary and unrefined. We agree that their methodological acumen has not been in statistics and experimental controls. But the three have been ingenious in devising new and effective procedures for collecting data that other theorists would have believed beyond the current powers of psychology. No personologist has made as big a contribution to the storehouse of personality tests as Murray. Allport pioneered techniques for comprehensively observing and rating the ongoing actions of subjects. And Maslow specialized in the clinical interpretation of natural records. Aside from the obvious intelligence and talent of these theorists, their methodological ingenuity can be traced to their humanistic conviction that any aspect of human behavior that is important is worth studying, even if it seems too private, internal, and elusive to the tough-minded scientist. Armed with this freeing sense of the importance of tracing down the innards of personality, however difficult that might be, Allport, Maslow, and Murray have been able to employ their gifts toward the creation of ingenious methods of obtaining personality data. Other comparably gifted researchers have been hampered in this regard by a narrowing view of what is science and what is not.

Specific Influences on Personality Research

It is possible to discern certain specific influences each of our three theorists has had on the research of others. Sometimes these others were students of the theorists, but sometimes the influence was more informal and indirect than that. Once again, do not expect an exhaustive listing of relevant research, for our aim is more modest than comprehensive.

ALLPORT'S INFLUENCE

Of the three theorists, Allport seems to have had the least impact on other researchers. This is perhaps understandable, as his approach stresses morphological or idiographic methods. Such methods are difficult to devise and usually require more time and effort to employ than do the ubiquitous nomothetic procedures. Especially because of this, one should avoid any overly simple conclusion that Allport's impact on personality research is less important than that of the other two theorists.

Allport (1962) has himself listed several morphogenic procedures that have been used in research. One procedure is the method of matching, in which the experimenter (or sometimes subjects, for that matter) have the task of fitting together any record of personal expression with any other record. In the accuracy of matching this case record with that test profile, or this handwriting with that voice, one can discover how much of a perceptible form quality saturates separate performances. One will recognize this as the procedure Allport and his collaborators employed in studies of expressive movement. As a method, it is suited to determining "the Johnian quality of

John." One of Allport's students, Estes (1938), employed this technique in further studies of expressive characteristics. In six experiments, Estes determined the ability of 323 judges to appraise the personalities of 15 male subjects from motion pictures of their nonverbal behavior in various settings. A different type of judge was employed in each experiment (for example, college students, adults, social workers). In general, it emerged that the nonverbal expressive movements in the motion pictures do permit inferences concerning personality that are more accurate than chance alone. It appears that some subjects are easier to judge than others, and that some judges are better at judging than others. Also, some kinds of judgments are easier to make, with overall assessments being more accurately made than are specific aspects of personality. The best judges, regardless of professional affiliation, tended to operate less conceptually in their thinking and to be more interested in painting and dramatics.

Allport has carried out several analogous studies (Allport and Cantril, 1934). Huntley (1940), another of Allport's students, even investigated the degree to which subjects could match their own protocols together, after a period of time had elapsed from when they were collected. Allport contends that in such uses of matching techniques one stands to learn more about the overall and unique pattern of a person's personality than in comparisons of performance to averages.

Another morphogenic procedure was devised by A. L. Baldwin (1942), also a student of Allport and now a prominent child developmental psychologist. Baldwin made use of a series of personal letters written by a woman named Jenny. The object of interest was Jenny's thought structure. Similarities of feeling tone across various topics were detected, so that functionally equivalent topics could be found. Similarly, Jenny's experiences were grouped together in order to further pinpoint her individuality. Baldwin calls this procedure "personal structure analysis," and carries it out without reference to general norms. More recently, yet another of Allport's students, Paige (1966), conducted a more technically sophisticated analysis of Jenny's letters. He used a computer procedure whereby each letter was analysed for the occurrence of a large number of categories of words. Correlations among all the categories were computed, and the resultant matrix was factor analysed. Eight factors were extracted which were interpreted as: aggression, possessiveness, affiliation, autonomy, familial acceptance, sexuality, sentience, and martyrdom. These factors provide a morphogenic depiction of Jenny.

Allport (1962) lists several other morphogenic and quasi-morphogenic techniques that have been used by other researchers. Among them are self-anchoring scales (Kilpatrick and Cantril, 1960), individualized questionnaires (Shapiro, 1961), Q sorts (Stephenson, 1953), the Role Repertory Test (Kelly, 1955), and inverse factor analysis.

Allport has also had an influence on the content of personality research even when morphogenic methodology has not been used. This influence is more difficult to discern, but there are several clear examples of it in the research of his students. In this regard, Wilson (1960) conducted research on the nature of religious experience—one of Allport's abiding concerns (1955, 1963). The touchstone for Wilson's study are the findings indicating that church-goers harbor more ethnic prejudice than nonchurch-goers.[1] In attempting to resolve this paradox, Allport has assumed that there are two forms of religious commitment, one that is *extrinsic* and another that is *intrinsic*. The extrinsic commitment, like all opportunistic functioning, involves religious devotion not as a value in its own right, but as an instrumental value serving the motives of personal comfort, security, or social status. The

---

1. See Argyle, 1960.

intrinsic, or propriate, commitment involves religious faith as a supreme value in its own right. Wilson constructed a questionnaire to measure these two orientations separately, and found them to be moderately but not highly correlated. In various samples of Protestant and Catholic church-goers, he found as expected that those with extrinsic orientations tended toward greater prejudice than those with intrinsic orientations. In a subtle additional analysis, Wilson found subjects who endorsed both intrinsic and extrinsic items on the questionnaire to be the most prejudiced of all. This suggests that an undifferentiated, "illogical," prereligious attitude is a special spawning ground of bigotry. Although this study does not permit full understanding of why even intrinsically oriented church-goers are more prejudiced than nonchurch-goers, it does begin to provide a basis for approaching this problem.

The general problem of prejudice is a frequent topic for research on the part of Allport's students. Pettigrew (1964), for example, has concerned himself for years with understanding the various forms of racial prejudice existing in the South. In his research, Pettigrew shows Allport's preference for detailed interview techniques and for distinguishing between habitual (or expressive) forms of discrimination and motivated (or dynamic) forms.

There are several other research topics of contemporary significance that bear rather directly on Allport's theoretical interests. But it is not at all clear that they exist through any direct influence of his, and therefore they will not be elaborated here. Suffice it to mention that the growing literature on internal versus external locus of control as a personality variable determining actions (Rotter, Seeman, and Liverant, 1966) can be readily interpreted in terms of Allport's distinction between proactive and reactive functioning. There are also studies seeming to bear on some of Allport's criteria of maturity.[2]

2. See Maddi, 1968.

MURRAY'S INFLUENCE

Murray has had an enormous direct influence on personality research. Partly this is due to the passage through his Psychological Clinic Annex (a unique collaborative research enterprise described in the following chapter) of more than two generations of personological leaders. But it is also due to his having formulated an eminently usable list of needs with which to describe persons, and pioneering several methods of personality measurement (Murray, 1938). Because there was nothing in his theorizing precluding the employment of nomothetic procedures, Murray's influence could be much more general than Allport's.

Murray's list of needs has had great impact on those personologists who construct tests for assessing personality. The list is comprehensive, concrete, and rigorous enough to render it a reasonable starting point in describing individual differences. One recent test of relevance is the *Activities Index,* which includes thirty of Murray's needs, each measured by ten questionnaire items (Stern, 1958a). Another test measuring needs is the *Edwards Personal Preference Schedule,* which employs a forced-choice format in presenting questions to the subject (Edwards, 1963). This hardly exhausts the tests that have built upon Murray's needs. Each test has its strong and weak points, but that is not our concern at present. The tests are in active use not only in research but in clinical diagnosis as well.

The availability of such tests for assessing personality has sparked their use in individual research studies too numerous to mention. In one representative study, subjects who had taken the Edwards Personal Preference Inventory were put through three experimental tasks requiring the explicit demonstration of dependent or independent behavior (Bernadin and Jessor, 1957). Those subjects who had scored high on the need for deference and low on the need for autonomy showed more reliance on others for approval and for help than did those subjects low on the need for deference and high on the need for autonomy. No relationship was found, however, between these need measures and conformity to the opinions and demands of others. This study suggests that knowing a person's need scores on the test should provide a reasonable basis for predicting his actions.

Bernadin and Jessor's study and the many others like it have assessed needs in structured self-description. In other words, the subject answers questions posed by the experimenter. The import of these questions are more or less clear. The subject knows he is describing himself. Although Murray himself used this kind of approach, he also advocated more unstructured, fantasy procedures. When asked to fantasize, the subject must provide his own structure and cannot be sure of what the experimenter wants or even that his task is to describe himself. One of Murray's techniques for eliciting fantasy, the *Thematic Apperception Test,* has come to be the second most popular test for clinical diagnosis (Murray, 1943). It has also been used widely in research as a means of assessing needs.

The most intensive and dramatic research theme using fantasy procedures is that of McClelland, his associates, and his students. McClelland, Atkinson, Clark, and Lowell (1953) concentrated on the need for achievement, provided a carefully devised scoring system for relevant thematic apperceptions, and concerned themselves with important psychometric properties of the resulting scores.

A great many studies of the construct validity of the need for achievement score have now been performed (Atkinson, 1958; McClelland, et al., 1953). One group of findings suggests the social and intellectual significance of need for achievement. American males with high need for achievement come more often from the middle class than from the lower or upper classes, have better memory for incompleted tasks when the situation is arranged so that everyone must complete and fail to complete an equal number of tasks, are more apt to volunteer as subjects for psychological experiments, are more active in college and community activites, choose experts over friends when asked who they want to work with on difficult problems, and are more resistant to social pressure to conform.

Another group of findings concerns the need for achievement and work situations (Atkinson, 1958; McClelland, et al., 1953). Several studies combine to suggest that high need for achievement will serve a person best when he perceives that he can display significant or personally relevant forms of excellence through his attempts. If the task is routine or if finishing it quickly implies either cooperating with someone or getting some nonachievement reward like time off, subjects low in need for achievement will perform better. In addition, it has been found that subjects high in need for achievement will, when given a choice, select moderate levels of risk rather than very low or very high risks (Atkinson, 1958). With low or high risks, success is either insured or accidental, neither of which would be attractive to the person highly in need of achievement. Having gained considerable understanding of the effects of need for achievement on individual behavior, McClelland (1961) then turned to the more general effect of average levels of this need in societies on their rate of economic growth. With a world-wide sample, McClelland was able to argue that the relationship is a positive one, and that the direction of causality is probably from the need to economic growth, not the other way around.

Similar though less extensive research has been mounted for the needs for affiliation and power (Atkinson, 1958), and the need for variety (Maddi, 1968, pp. 435–43). It must be said of all this research that Murray would be somewhat disconcerted to find single needs selected and studied. His emphasis has always been more on the confluence of needs that comprise a total personality. Nonetheless, his theorizing and research were clearly a direct influence on the research that has been mentioned.

More dear to Murray's heart is a comprehensive study of a few persons, with consideration of many needs and application of several measurement procedures. Such research has been mounted by some of his students and associates, such as Mac-Kinnon (1965), and Stein (1963). It is not surprising that personologists who do research of this sort tend to found research institutes, for the repeated and extensive testing of subjects is greatly facilitated by having a center at which the subjects can be made to feel somewhat at home, and can even be boarded.

MASLOW'S INFLUENCE

Surprisingly, a major recent influence of Maslow's thinking has been upon organization research. Of special relevance in this context has been his conception of need-hierarchy. Cross-sectional research has produced results suggesting the plausibility of this conception. For example, Davis (1946) discovered that workers from underprivileged backgrounds lacked ambition or concern for the nature of their work. These workers are presumably still attempting to satisfy physiological and safety needs, and therefore cannot consider the dignity of their performance. Along similar lines, Pellegrin and Coates (1957) found that executives are likely to define success as career accomplishments, whereas first-level superiors (presumably with less achievement satisfaction) tend to view success in terms of security and income. Further, Porter (1963) found that high executives are more concerned with esteem and self-actualization than are managers with lower status in an organization. The results reported by Centers (1948), Morse and Weiss (1955), Lyman (1955), and Veroff, Atkinson, Feld, and Gurin (1960) can be similarly interpreted.

The main difficulty with these studies of need-hierarchy is

that they are cross-sectional, relying for their conclusions on comparisons of different groups within an organization. The crucial test of Maslow's need-hierarchy would require a longitudinal design, because the conception states that as a lower level need becomes progressively satisfied the next higher level need increases. As Hall and Nougaim (1968) point out, the results mentioned above might be showing no more than that persons with high self-actualization needs tend to be selected for executive positions, and persons with security and physiological needs for less responsible positions. If the differential in needs existed prior to job selection, then the relevance of the need-hierarchy conception as an explanation of organizational accomplishment would be small. Hall and Nougaim carried out a carefully planned longitudinal study in which it was possible to determine whether the satisfaction of lower level needs was coincident with the emergence of higher level needs within each subject. Various subjective measures of need satisfaction and strength were derived from interviews (a procedure of which Maslow would have approved), and an objective measure of satisfaction was also included for completeness. In this study there was no support for the need-hierarchy conception. It remains now for further investigation to clarify the precise meaning of the discrepancy between this study and the others mentioned. But doubt has certainly been cast by this well-designed study on the causal implications of Maslow's thinking in an organizational setting.

Recently, Shostrom (1965, 1966) has introduced a questionnaire, called the *Personal Orientation Inventory,* that purports to measure variables of concern to Maslow. The test consists of 150 pairs of items in a forced-choice format that yields two overall scores. One of the overall scores is *Inner Directed Support,* or the degree to which one is his own source of support, and the other is *Time Competence,* or the degree to which one lives in the present. In addition, there are ten subscales measuring self-actualizing values, existentiality, feeling reactivity, spontaneity, self-regard, self-acceptance, nature of man, synergy, acceptance of aggression, and capacity for intimate contact. High reliability has been reported for the various scales (Shostrom, 1966; Klavetter and Mogar, 1967; Ilardi and May, 1968).

The rapidly accumulating evidence for the Personal Orientation Inventory's validity has been reviewed by Shostrom (1966), Fox, Knapp, and Michael (1968), and Guinan and Foulds (1970). These validity studies, several of which will be mentioned here, fall into four areas: comparison of clinical groups with regard to test scores, use of the test in understanding the effects of various psychotherapies, the relationship of the test to other tests, and various behaviors as a function of test scores.

In comparing clinical groups with regard to test scores, Personal Orientation Inventory scales have been found to discriminate between groups nominated by clinicians as self-actualized and nonself-actualized (Shostrom, 1965); between felons and normals (Fisher, 1968); and between hospitalized psychiatric patients on the one hand and samples designated self-actualized, normal, and nonself-actualized but unhospitalized on the other hand (Fox, Knapp, and Michael, 1968). In a sample of normal adults being trained as counselors, Personal Orientation Inventory scales correlated positively with self-actualizing ratings made by supervisors, group process leaders, and clinical psychologists involved in the training (McClain, 1970).

Also of interest is the Personal Orientation Inventory's relationship to psychotherapy treatments. In a comparison of matched therapy groups at a beginning and advanced stage of therapy, Shostrom and Knapp (1966) found the test's scales discriminated the groups in the expected direction. Personal Orientation Inventory scores were also found to increase for a group of persons in a marathon group, while a control group showed no such changes (Guinan and Foulds, 1970). Other studies have reported similar findings (Byrd, 1967; Culbert, Clark, and Bobele, 1968).

One can get further insight into the meaning of this test by studying the relationship of Personal Orientation Inventory scores to scores on other tests. Negative correlations have been found between Personal Orientation Inventory scores and the Depression and Hypochondriasis scales of the Minnesota Multiphasic Personality Inventory (Shostrom and Knapp, 1966), as well as the Neuroticism scale of the Eysenck Personality Inventory (Knapp, 1965). The Inner Directed Support scale of the Personal Orientation Inventory shows a negative correlation with the abasement scale and a positive correlation with the autonomy scale of the Edwards Personal Preference Inventory (Grossack, Armstrong, and Lussieu, 1966). Finally, positive correlations have been found between the Maslovian test and various tests reflecting creativity (Braun and Asta, 1968).

A final group of findings concerns nontest behaviors. The Personal Orientation Inventory scores show a positive relationship to academic achievement (Steward, 1968), to teaching effectiveness (Dandes, 1966), to the effectiveness of dormitory assistants (Graff and Bradshaw, 1970), and to the ability of psychotherapists to be facilitative to patients (Foulds, 1969). The Inner Directed Support scale also discriminates achieving from underachieving college freshmen matched for aptitude and other variables (LeMay and Damm, 1968).

It would seem that the Personal Orientation Inventory is a useful test of self-actualization as an expression of robust mental health. This conclusion is justified even after a study of the test's fakeability. Braun and LaFars (1969) had groups of subjects take the test under different instructions and found that scores were not enhanced by attempts either to make a good impression or appear well adjusted. Only when subjects were given specific knowledge of self-actualization theory and of the test itself were they successful in faking good scores. It must be concluded that the Personal Orientation Inventory is a promising test, has sparked considerable research interest, and is clearly a direct influence of Maslow.

Indirect Influences on Research

Without a doubt, Allport, Maslow, and Murray have had considerable impact on personality research out of their shared humanistic orientation. While this impact is difficult to pinpoint, it cannot be denied. We believe that the current research emphases on creativity and originality rather than mere intelligence, normal subjects rather than pathological ones, and comprehensive though difficult procedures for collecting data, can be traced in no small measure to the general impact of these three theorists. And the trend toward humanism in personality research is apparently accelerating. Before long we can expect to see even more emphasis upon love and cooperation rather than anxiety and competitiveness, future-orientations rather than past-orientations, and a psychology of the possible rather than the actual.

6

The Men Behind the Theories

There is probably no viable way to theorize about personality without in some fashion relying fairly extensively on your own personality. After all, one's perceptions, sensibilities, memories, interpretations, and evaluations of experience, whether it come from the laboratory or more naturalistically, are unavoidably influenced by one's personality. And one's personality is, in turn, shaped by the experiences comprising one's developmental past. A perusal of the lives of the men behind the theories we are here considering is more, therefore, than simple human interest. It constitutes another way of approaching an understanding of the theories themselves.

Early Life

Gordon Allport was born in Montezuma, Indiana in 1897. He was the youngest of four brothers. His father was a country doctor who had gone into medicine shortly before Allport was born after a career in business. It is probable that Gordon and his mother were his father's first patients. Soon the family moved to a small town in Ohio, where they stayed for the next twelve years.

Allport, considerably younger than his brothers, felt forced

to adopt a separate way of life. He felt like an isolate, quick
with words, poor at games, but finally the center of a small
cluster of friends. He graduated from high school second in his
class, regarding himself as ". . . a good routine student, but
definitely uninspired and uncurious about anything beyond the
usual adolescent concerns" (Allport, 1968, p. 379). Apparently unsure of his intellectual future, he decided to apply to
Harvard at the last minute on the urging of his brother, Floyd,
a Harvard graduate himself. Gordon barely passed the entrance
examination but was finally admitted.

The general family atmosphere in which Gordon Allport
spent his childhood and early adolescence is probably best
typified as "plain Protestant piety and hard work" (ibid., p.
379). Vacations and leisure were rare, with hard work tem-
His mother, who had been a schoolteacher, imbued her sons
with the importance of knowledge and of searching for ultimate
religious answers to the problems of life. Since his father lacked
adequate hospital facilities and personnel, Gordon and other
members of the family regularly helped by tending the office,
washing bottles, and generally dealing with patients. All four
brothers were from early age trained "in the practical urgencies
of life as well as in a broad humanitarian outlook" (ibid., p.
379). Vacations and leisure were rare, with hard work tempered by trust and affection marking family life. To a strong
degree, Allport was schooled in the importance of public service and responsibility to others.

Abraham Maslow started life in 1908 in Brooklyn, New
York. His mother and father were both uneducated immigrants,
leading marginal lives in the United States, and hoping fer-
vently for something better for their son. Though uneducated,
Maslow's father must have had great drive and persistence,
having "thumbed his way across the whole continent of Europe
from Russia and got here by the age of 15" (Maslow, 1968c,
p. 37).

The warmth and encouragement Maslow received from his

parents must have been in glaring contrast to his reception from the others around him.

> With my childhood, it's a wonder I'm not psychotic. I was a little Jewish boy in the non-Jewish neighborhood. It was a little like being the first Negro enrolled in the all-white school. I was isolated and unhappy. I grew up in libraries and among books, without friends. (Maslow, 1968c, p. 37)

Apparently, both Allport and Maslow felt isolated as youngsters, and relied upon intellectual pursuits in an attempt to find a place in the sun. But Allport was, by virtue of his Protestant, professional family background, in a more socially central position than Maslow, the little son of uneducated Jewish immigrants. Whereas Allport was schooled by his parents to be socially useful and responsible, Maslow was encouraged to be a success, to nullify the marginal status his parents could not avoid saddling him with. Both youngsters were taught to shun idleness, but self-interested endeavor would have come more easily to Maslow than Allport. Indeed, whereas Maslow's intellectualism incorporated from the start a scrappy aggressiveness, Allport's was more consistent with cultural conventions, if no less incisive.

This is not to say that, in adulthood, Maslow was more self-interested than Allport. Actually, both men had a deep sense of service to their fellow men. But this sentiment emanated from different early experiences. Allport was taught it directly, as a value his parents espoused and which the whole family practiced toward the patients, those people less fortunate than they. In contrast, Maslow must have identified personally with the unfortunates, being one himself. Through the suffering inflicted upon him by the advantaged, non-Jewish people around him, Maslow must have learned the horror of helplessness. Thus the wish to help people to live better could have had its origins in his wish to live better himself.

If there was any difference in the quality of the commitment to public service felt by both Allport and Maslow, it involved a greater distrust of others on Maslow's part. Allport was consistently unwilling to believe in evil propensities in man, whereas Maslow recognized these qualities but staunchly maintained that there was a more constructive alternative. This difference is understandable if one recognizes that Maslow may well have suffered at the hands of others in early years more than did Allport.

Henry Murray was born in 1893 in a brownstone home on the present site of Rockefeller Center in New York City. He lived there throughout his childhood and adolescence, spending his summers on Long Island near the sea. This period was punctuated by four rather lengthy trips to Europe, "during the course of which [he] compliantly dragged his feet through most of the great museums, cathedrals, and historic buildings between Naples and the Highlands of Scotland" (Murray, 1967, p. 298). In speaking of his father, Murray says:

> My father was a Scot, born near Melbourne, Australia, where his father, a British Army officer, was sent and stationed until he died a few years after his fourth son's birth. This son, my father, was about one when he and his mother rounded the tempestuous Cape in a schooner, with cascades of ocean pouring into their cabin, and eventually arrived in England as destitute relatives of some studbook uncles and cousins who were not inclined to be disturbed beyond using their influence to get my father entered at the famous "bluecoat" charity school in London, Christ's Hospital, where Coleridge, Leigh Hunt, and Lamb had studied. . . . After his mother's premature death my father, a penniless orphan without a college education, came by way of Toronto to New York City. His anonymous arrival must have been as different as it could have been from that of his great-grandfather, the flamboyant and irascible Earl of Dunmore, who a hundred years earlier, [had been] sent there . . . as Governor of Virginia, where he lived in that grand mansion at Williamsburg which we can see today in a restored state. (Murray, 1967, p. 295)

Murray's father soon married the lively daughter of a man who was to become quite wealthy. Thus, Murray's historically aristocratic family was supplied again with money. It is also clear that Murray's mother was of upper-class background, her ancestors having come here in the early days before independence, and having had an intimate relationship to important social developments ever since. Murray is especially articulate concerning the personalities of his parents and the family atmosphere they created:

If, as countless philosophers have held, happiness, resulting from this or that variety of conduct, is the only state that a rational man will endeavor to secure, then my father was as successful as anybody I could name, provided one correlates happiness with a continuing state of unperturbed serenity, cheerfulness, enjoyment of sheer being, trust, and mutual affection, or, in other words, a life of moderate, solid, predictable satisfactions, free from choler, anxiety, guilt, and shame . . . my father, though not installed as a charismatic hero, was always a positive univalent figure in my mind, a dependable guide and teacher in the Hellenic mode, rather than a threatening, awesome, high and mighty judge. . . . It was my mother who was the ambivalent person: more often the focus of attention, affection, and concern than my father was, year in and year out, but also more resented now and then, mostly for correcting my abominable manners, for nagging about minutiae, or for enforcing duties or requesting services which interrupted my activities. Of the two, she was the more energetic, restless, enthusiastic, enterprising, and talkative —giving us daily reports of her personal preoccupations, her doings, encounters, worries, and frustrations—also the more changeable, moody, and susceptible to melancholy. I resemble my mother in all but one of these respects: like my fortunate father, I have never been plagued by endogenous anxieties and worries, and, like him again, I adopted at a very early age the role of physician to these perturbations in my mother and later to comparable but slighter perturbations in my more rational and steady wife. (Murray, 1967, pp. 296–97)

Clearly, Murray led a life of relative ease, free from want and a sense of helplessness. The people around him, and the experiences to which he was privy, were at the most sophisticated and tasteful levels our culture could provide. In this regard, it is interesting that Murray claims his psychoanalysis could uncover little or no resentment and hostility toward his parents.

Henry Murray was the middle of three children, spaced apart from each other by a bit over three years. The eldest was "a fascinating, mischievous daughter with flashes of ungovernable temper, followed by two more easily manageable sons, me in the middle and my brother, the cute kid, with a repertoire of precocious tricks indicative of real brilliance in the future" (Murray, 1967, p. 297). The feelings of anger toward his sister that are described by Murray do not seem especially out of the ordinary. And he seems to have related famously to his brother.

In depicting his youth, Murray rather characteristically understates that "on the whole [I seem] to have grown up as an average privileged American boy of that era (before the days of automobiles, motorboats, movies, and all that), with an identity in the eyes of [my] miniature social surround which could not be captured in terms of either docile or rebellious, timid or reckless, awkward or agile, dull or bright, hopeless or promising, in or out" (Murray, 1967, p. 298). Although he does seem to have been slow to develop intellectually, Murray was certainly exposed throughout his childhood to the varied and sophisticated experiences of the well-born. Just one of the many testaments to this is that the mother, father, and three children constituting the Murray family employed seven servants.

Murray's high school years were spent at Groton, an elite finishing school in New England, where his Republican, conservative, upper-class beginnings were continued. This trend continued through the college years, which Murray spent at Harvard.

There is little in Murray's early life of the suffering and socially marginal status that led Maslow to a concern for improving the quality of living, or of the religious ideologies and practical activities that led Allport to a similar commitment. In Murray's case, an interest in social improvement seems to have been based on two physical defects, plus some of the more usual experiences of failure that mark childhood. Murray had an internal strabismus (or inward turning) of one eye, which, through faulty correction, became an external strabismus (or outward turning). This disorder, though slight, was sufficient to interfere with stereoscopic vision, rendering him physically unsure and relatively poor at games. Murray believes this disorder and its attendant psychological insecurities to have contributed to, if not to have caused, his stuttering. This second defect seems to have added to the insecurities fostered by the first.

The immediate effect of these two physical defects was to spur young Murray to excel physically. He played quarterback in football and won a featherweight boxing championship at primary school. A more general consequence seems to have been to establish high standards of excellence for intellectual and interpersonal endeavors as well. Murray's attempt to contribute to the improvement of life in general, which matches the attempts of Allport and Maslow, can be understood as a generalization of his attempt to transcend his two physical defects. Of course, the high level of sophistication characteristic of the Murray household established habits, values, and expectations as to what life could be for everyone.

Intellectual Formation

A general commitment to serve mankind by investigating how individual and social life could be improved, present in

Allport, Maslow, and Murray by virtue of certain aspects of their beginnings, was deepened and rendered more specific by the experiences of higher education. This period of intellectual formation is indispensable to an understanding of how these three men came to be personologists and to take a position of leadership in the more humanistic strain within that field.

Gordon Allport, as has already been said, followed his older brother to Harvard College, where he spent the years from 1915 through 1919. This was a time of tremendous awakening, broadening, and deepening of intellect for him. In depicting his overwhelming initial experience, he says:

> Did ever a Midwestern lad receive a greater impact from "going East to college?" I doubt it. Almost overnight my world was remade. My basic moral values, to be sure, had been fashioned at home. What was new was the horizon of intellect and culture I was now invited to explore. . . . First and foremost was the pervading sense of high standards. . . . At the first hour examinations I received an array of D's and C's. Profoundly shattered, I stiffened my efforts and ended the year with A's. . . . In the course of fifty years' association with Harvard I have never ceased to admire the unspoken expectation of excellence. (Allport, 1968b, p. 380)

However overwhelmed Allport must have been by the sophistication of Harvard, his keen sense of duty and hard work served him well in applying himself toward meeting the high intellectual standards he so amply respected.

It is hardly surprising that one of Allport's major fields of study at college was Social Ethics. His initial interest in this field, nurtured in his home, was hardly discouraged by such teachers as James Ford. Nor is it surprising that Allport, so habituated to practical social service, would have conducted, all through his college years, a boys' club in the West End of Boston.

At various times I did volunteer visiting for the Family Society and served as volunteer probation officer. During one summer I held a paid job with the Humane Society of Cleveland; during another I worked for Professor Ford as field agent for the registration of homes for war workers in crowded industrial cities of the East. At the Phillips Brooks House I held a paid job as executive of the Cosmopolitan Club. All this social service was deeply satisfying, partly because it gave me a feeling of competence (to offset a generalized inferiority feeling) and partly because I found I liked to help people with their problems. (Allport, 1968b, pp. 381–82)

In the last sentence, Allport makes clear that the inferiority feeling presumably generated in the family by his position as the decidedly youngest son and the habits and identification fostered by his physician father were still operative in college.

While in college, Allport also developed an abiding interest in psychology. The roots of this interest are a little less clear than those of the concern with social ethics. To be sure, psychology, especially the emphasis on personality, deals considerably with the kinds of questions posed in ethics: the personologist is, after all, concerned with what makes the good life, and how to foster it in people. In addition, Allport's older brother, Floyd, was at the time a graduate student in psychology at Harvard, and encouraged Gordon to take courses in his department. In any event, it should be noted that although Allport studied psychology, he was not committed during his undergraduate years to a career in that field. Indeed, he records of his first course with Munsterberg that while he was intellectually stimulated by experimental psychology, he was perplexed by the chill of the hard-line, atomistic approach usual in that subject matter. But by the time he graduated, Allport had taken psychology courses with some fine teachers, among them Edwin B. Holt, Leonard Troland, Walter Dearborn, Ernest Southard, and Herbert Langfeld. He had also served as a subject in his brother's doctoral research.

World War I interfered only slightly with Allport's studies; he was permitted to continue his studies while serving as an inductee in the Student's Army Training Corps. By this time, he was beginning to think like a psychologist, even to the point of writing on the psychological aspects of rifle practice. The new interest in psychology merged with the older one in social ethics. This can be seen as a gradual process of secularization; he was attempting to achieve a mature religious position by "replacing childhood conceptions of doctrine with some sort of humanitarian religion" (Allport, 1968b, p. 382). "Arrogance in psychological theorizing has always antagonized me; I believe it is better to be tentative, eclectic, and humble. . . . If one were to do effective social service, one needed a sound conception of human personality" (ibid.).

Allport was unsure, after graduation, whether to settle on social service administration or teaching, but gave the latter a chance when an opportunity occurred. While teaching in Constantinople, he was offered and accepted a fellowship for graduate study of psychology at Harvard, thereby effectively making the decision for an academic career.

Allport visited Freud en route to the United States. Their encounter clearly typifies Allport's approach to personality, and presaged his abiding opposition to depth psychology. As the interview began, Freud sat in silence, waiting to be told the reason for the meeting. Says Allport:

> I was not prepared for silence and had to think fast to find a suitable conversational gambit. I told him of an episode on the tram car on my way to his office. A small boy about four years of age had displayed a conspicuous dirt phobia. He kept saying to his mother, "I don't want to sit there . . . don't let that dirty man sit beside me." To him everything was *schmutz*. His mother was a well-starched *Hausfrau,* so dominant and purposive looking that I thought the cause and effect apparent. . . . When I finished my story Freud fixed his kindly therapeutic eyes upon me and said, "And was that little boy you?" Flabbergasted and feel-

ing a bit guilty, I contrived to change the subject. While Freud's misunderstanding of my motivation was amusing, it also started a deep train of thought. I realized that he was accustomed to neurotic defenses and that my manifest motivation (a sort of rude curiosity and youthful ambition) escaped him. For therapeutic progress he would have to cut through my defenses, but it so happened that therapeutic progress was not here an issue. . . . This experience taught me that depth psychology, for all its merits, may plunge too deep, and that psychologists would do well to give full recognition to manifest motives before probing the unconscious. (Allport, 1968b, p. 383)

Was Freud right? Perhaps, in the sense that Allport's proper, moral, religious upbringing produced in him a disdain for conflict, disorder, the seamy side of life, while simultaneously instilling the kind of intense ambition that could lead to visiting a great man without having any special purpose in mind except a meeting. In that sense, Allport was the little boy. Allport may well have realized this to some degree, as his feeling of guilt suggests, but he also felt misunderstood. For him, the main reason for his visit was "rude curiosity and youthful ambition," not the imputed intellectualized reaction formation against dirtying himself by talking to the eminent psychopathologist. In any event, the episode highlights the emphasis of Allport's later theorizing on the conscious, observable, tangible aspects of personality, to the relative exclusion of conflicts, anxieties, and defenses.

Allport seems to have been unchallenged and a bit bored with his studies in graduate school. He also had vocational misgivings, some of which were dispelled when Langfeld, his teacher, encouraged him to find his own way in psychology. With some trepidation he did just this, and his doctoral dissertation ". . . was perhaps the first American dissertation written explicitly on the question of component traits of personality" (Allport, 1968b, p. 385). His dissertation committee included not only Langfeld and Ford, but McDougall as well.

The latter must be counted among the important influences on Allport during this period. Foreshadowing what was to come later from colleagues, criticism of the dissertation was immediate and ample, and the young Allport had to face the dissatisfaction of respected authorities. Titchener, at a conference, was very disapproving of Allport's approach, but continued support from Landfeld saved the day.

> The whole experience was a turning point. Never since that time have I been troubled by rebukes or professional slights directed at my maverick interests. Later, of course, the field of personality became not only acceptable but highly fashionable. (Allport, 1968b, p. 385)

Allport's early intellectual career seems to have been somewhat conforming. It expressed the themes rendered important for him by his family atmosphere. Through practice and accumulation of knowledge, however, the intellectualism shaped by early experience became vigorous and capable enough to become independent—its own source of standards. In this personal development, the concept of functional autonomy of motives, so crucial to Allport's theorizing, is presaged.

Two other important things happened during Gordon Allport's graduate years. He met his future wife, a fellow graduate student from Boston, who, after taking her Master's Degree, worked in clinical psychology. Their interests were parallel, and a long, stable relationship was begun. The Allports married in 1925 and had a son in 1927. This son later became a pediatrician, recapitulating his grandfather's career.

Another event of particular note was Allport's receipt of a Sheldon Traveling Fellowship, which gave him two rich years in Europe. Armed with the Ph.D. he had received in 1922, Allport encountered Gestalt psychology in the persons of Max Wertheimer and Wolfgang Köhler. He also studied with Stumpf, Spranger, William Stern, and Heinz Werner, and was helped with his halting German by a fellow student, Heinrich

Klüver. Allport quickly recognized the German emphasis on holism as the intellectual support he needed for his own orientation toward personality, which was far removed from anything that could be reconciled with the associationistic ideology of Hume in which Allport had been reared. In addition, Allport was strongly influenced by the German doctrine of types. Allport spent the second year of his European sojourn in England, talking with Bartlett and I. S. Richards, but mainly cogitating upon and digesting the agreeable but heavy intellectual diet of the German academy.

At the end of the two years, Allport returned to Harvard, where Ford arranged an instructorship for him in social ethics. Besides offering Ford's course in this field, Allport also introduced a course in the psychology of personality—which may well have been the first in American higher education.

Maslow's higher education began with an attempt to specialize in law in response to pressure from his father. But this did not prove a meaningful area of study, for Maslow wanted to help man discover the basis for constructive, cooperative action rather than indulge the competitive, litigative side of him. When Maslow stated that law was not a suitable field for him, his father reluctantly accepted his son's wish to undertake a broad and eclectic course of study. For the elder Maslow, earning one's way and seeking power were the important things, whereas the son wanted to seek answers to rather deeper questions than those posed by routine professional careerism.

While still in high school, at the tender age of 16, Maslow fell in love with Bertha, the girl he would soon marry. Maslow's father did not understand his son's interest in such an early marriage, but, while articulately opposed, was eventually compliant.

In an attempt to circumvent the strained relationship with his father, Maslow left New York to pursue his studies at Cornell. He transferred again to Wisconsin for his junior and senior years where he was joined by Bertha. They married when he was 20 and she 19. From the first meeting, Maslow reports being so taken with her that, though extremely shy, he "tagged along after her" (Maslow, 1968c, p. 37). Getting married seems to have been extremely important to the young Maslow, giving him a greater sense of worth and purpose and direction than before. This is aptly summarized in his statement that "life didn't really start for me until I got married and went to Wisconsin" (Maslow, 1968c, p. 37).

A major reason for Maslow's return to Wisconsin was the behaviorism of J. B. Watson:

> I had discovered J. B. Watson and I was sold on behaviorism. It was an explosion of excitement for me. . . . Bertha came to pick me up and I was dancing down Fifth Avenue with exuberance; I embarrassed her, but I was so excited about Watson's program. It was beautiful.
>
> I was confident that here was a real road to travel, solving one problem after another and changing the world. . . . I was off to Wisconsin to change the world. But off to Wisconsin because of a lying catalog. I went there to study with Koffka, the psychologist; Dreisch, the biologist; and Meiklejohn, the philosopher.
>
> When I showed up on the campus, they weren't there. They had just been visiting professors, but the school put them in the catalog anyway. (Maslow, 1968c, p. 37)

One can imagine the intense disappointment of this poor, disadvantaged, scrappy young man, who might have been more skeptical of a catalog from the very beginning if he had been more sophisticated or less needy. But Maslow did not indulge disappointment long, making his way somehow and continuing to develop intellectually.

> Oh, but I was so lucky, though. I was young Harry Helson's first Ph.D. And they were angels, my professors. I've always had angels around. They helped me when I needed it; fed me; Bill Sheldon taught me how to buy a suit. I didn't know anything of amenities. Edward L. Thorndike was an angel to me. Clark Hull was another. (Maslow, 1968c, p. 37).

Maslow, unlike Allport, seems to have specialized in psychology from the beginning of college work. At least, there is nothing in his writing about his past to suggest a conflict about vocation. While studying under Helson at Wisconsin, Maslow did an observational study of reproduction in monkeys; this subsequently became his doctoral dissertation. He said with humor, "Oh, I made a great discovery in my doctoral dissertation. Only somebody discovered it two months before me" (Maslow, 1968c, p. 37). Be that as it may, this study marks Maslow's beginnings in an abiding, consuming interest in sexuality and affection.

Maslow tried out the various approaches of his teachers, worked with them for a while, and then rejected them or adapted them to his own needs. He was hungry for understanding and for techniques of effective functioning in a world that must have seemed strange to him. He studied monkeys with Helson, but then generalized his conclusions about sex to humans, never to study monkeys again. Maslow's early interest in behaviorism as a way to help people perform and act better paled when his developing mind could not reconcile with his own experience the oversimplifications he sensed.

I didn't question [behaviorism] until I began reading Freud and Gestalt psychology and organismic psychology and studying the Rorschach test. At the same time, I stumbled into embryology and I read Ludwig von Bertalanffy's *Modern Theories of Development*. And I had become disillusioned with Bertrand Russell and with English philosophy generally. . . . I fell in love with Alfred North Whitehead and Henri Bergson. Their writing, their thinking destroyed behaviorism without my recognizing it.

Then when my baby was born that was the thunderclap that settled things. I looked at this tiny, mysterious thing and felt so stupid. I was stunned by the mystery and by the sense of not really being in control. I felt small and weak and feeble before all this. I'd say that anyone who had a baby couldn't be a behaviorist. . . . Behavioristic confidence and its attendant lack of humility reminds me of a child who is playing with atomic bombs. (Maslow, 1968c, p. 55)

In this statement, Maslow makes clear that not only his formal classes and teachers determined the course of his development in the college and graduate years. It became clear to him that persons could not really be molded and changed in the way behaviorism contended and that even if they could he would not want to do it. Maslow had found the intellectual foundations for his later humanistic views.

Personal experiences during this period certainly had an enormous effect on Maslow's future commitments. Indeed, in answering a question about the kind of education he would advocate for a bright young man nowadays, Maslow said:

Well, if I think of the great educational experiences of my life, the ones that taught me most, then it would be those that taught me the kind of person I was: the experiences that drew me out, strengthened me, made me taller and stronger. Psychoanalysis, for instance, was a big thing for me. And getting married. Marriage is a school itself . . . [also] having children. . . . Becoming a father changed my whole life, it taught me as if by revelation. And reading particular books. William Graham Sumner's *Folkways* was a Mt. Everest in my life. It changed me.

And my teachers were the best in the world. I sought them out; Erich Fromm, Karen Horney, Ruth Benedict, Max Wertheimer, Alfred Adler, David Levy and Harry Harlow. I was there in New York when the wave of distinguished emigres arrived from Europe. (Maslow, 1968c, p. 57).

Maslow, like Allport, apparently felt that, from the days of graduate school on, the formative intellectual experiences were informal, personal, and self-sought, rather than part of formal education. It is significant that Maslow gives marriage and parenthood such an important place, as his wife is apparently a strong woman with some considerable sense of what she wants in life. Relating to such a wife can undoubtedly be a growth-promoting developmental experience. Maslow seems also to have been a very involved and devoted father to his two daughters.

Interestingly enough, both Allport and Maslow encountered and rejected behaviorism in their early intellectual lives. Allport's rejection was easier and more rapid, because his home life had schooled him in an ethic that was humanistic despite its self-abnegating, Puritan flavor. In Munsterberg's course, Allport had difficulty understanding why such a cold approach would be taken. Had it not been for the encouragements of brother Floyd, one senses that Allport would have rejected behaviorism even sooner and more summarily than he did. Maslow, in contrast, had little by way of relevant ideologies to guide his peregrinations in psychology. Therefore, he toyed with behaviorism, the dominant force in psychology those days, with more seriousness and at greater length. In the end, however, he too rejected it as too analytic and cold and insufficiently concerned with the most human aspects of man. Both Allport and Maslow were profoundly influenced by Gestalt psychology, which emphasized holism and organismic structure.

In describing his college and graduate school years, Murray (1968) makes clear that his was truly an unusual life. He grew up in the lap of luxury, never attending public schools. After Groton, Murray went to Harvard College, graduating with an A.B. in history in 1915. While at college he received below average grades, perhaps because of an "unremitting youthful passion for athletic achievement" (Murray, 1968, p. 287). Because athletics were difficult for him, due to his lateral strabismus, he spent a good deal of time practicing. One of Murray's proudest achievements in those days was making the Harvard rowing team. On the day after a Harvard-Yale rowing match, he proposed marriage to Josephine L. Rantoul of Boston, whom he had ardently courted for three years. She accepted and the marriage began a long and stable intimacy that was very important to him.

Following graduation from Harvard, Murray entered the Columbia College of Physicians and Surgeons, from which he graduated at the head of his class in 1919. Then came an M.A. in biology from Columbia and brief service as an instructor of physiology at Harvard. The next step in his varied early career was a two-year surgical internship at Presbyterian Hospital in New York City. He then joined the Rockefeller Institute for Medical Research in New York. As a research assistant there, he continued research he had begun some years before on the biochemical aspects of various embryological phenomena. Then came a year of study at Cambridge University, where he obtained a Ph.D. in biochemistry in 1927. On the basis of these facts alone, it is strange that Murray, at the age of 33, never having completed a psychology course in his life, accepted an appointment at Harvard in 1927 as assistant to the famous psychopathologist Morton Prince.

One does not switch fields so dramatically without there being a complex story behind the simple facts. Murray, fortunately, has been quite explicit about the themes and influences culminating in his embracing psychology. In college and early medical school days, he seems to have had an aversion to formal psychology (Murray, 1968). He began Munsterberg's course at the same time as Allport did, but countenanced it even less. A medical school course in psychiatry and a perusal of Freud's *Interpretation of Dreams* apparently did not help. But all the while, lurking in the background, was a great sensitivity to and an interest in people which had its start in his childhood when he adopted his father's nurturant attitude toward his mother, and was intensified by an awareness of his own physical disability (ibid., p. 287–88). This sensitivity was expressed in his early intellectual career by his interest in history, biography, and literature. He was especially taken with Herman Melville, whom he was fond of calling "that alienated genius" (ibid., p. 287). Though generally at peace and emotionally stable, Murray feels he was drawn to people and characters of restless, aliented stamp due to an underlying and unexpressed propensity for melancholy.

The young Murray was trying very hard to find himself. Was he merely a pampered, conservative, dilettante son of wealth, capable of achieving through his own independent efforts a broader perspective on the human condition? Or was he a man of the people?

While interning at Presbyterian Hospital, Murray was struck "by the patients in mental hospitals whose expressions of emotion [seemed] more naturally human and appealing than the perfunctory, official behavior of the tired doctors" and was on many occasions "astonished, stimulated, and instructed by Dr. George Draper's pinpoint observations and brilliant intuitive diagnoses of patients with what was later to be called psychosomatic illness" (Murray, 1968, p. 288). As time went on, Murray

> spent more time than was considered proper for a surgeon inquisitively seeking psychogenic factors in my patients. Whatever I succeeded in doing for some of them—the dope fiend, the sword-swallower, the prostitute, the gangster—was more than repaid when, after leaving the hospital, they took me through their haunts in the underworld. This was psychology in the rough, but at least it prepared me to recognize the similarity between downtown doings and uptown dreams.

Even Murray's mentors provoked psychological thinking in him, for he came to believe that the strongly contended, contradictory theories of medicine they espoused were expressions at least in part of their personalities. In hopes of clarifying the personal basis of conceptual preferences, Murray sent a questionnaire to fifty creative thinkers, and arranged to take philosophy courses with Morris Cohen and Broad.

Although Murray was then and has remained deeply committed to research, he began to be dissatisfied with his biochemical, embryological studies:

From 1923 to 1926, during which span [my] bonds of affinity
with the creative processes in chicken embryos were step-wise
disengaged and attached to the germinal affects of human beings,
the actualizations [I] experienced were in part mentational but
predominantly emotional. Through [my] hospital activities, [my]
emotions had been engaged in empathizing with the somatic dis-
comforts and anxieties of each patient, especially on the female
ward; but these involvements were necessarily brief and super-
ficial, and when it came to chicken embryos, lovely as they were,
the opportunities for empathy were critically curtailed. In short,
in view of the profound affectional upheaval that swept [me] into
the unruly domain of psychology—the thereby down the pecking
order of the sciences—I am assuming . . . that up to that time an
assemblage of emotional potentialities had been denied adequate
participation in [my] work. (Murray, 1968, p. 290)

It was at this point in his emotional transition from surgery
to psychology that Murray encountered Carl Jung. The first
step was through reading:

The notion that science is the creative product of an engagement
between the scientist's psyche and the events to which he is at-
tentive prepared [me] for an enthusiastic embracement of Jung's
Psychological Types on the very day of its timely publication in
New York (1923) . . . this book . . . came to [me] as a gratuitous
answer to an unspoken prayer. Among other things, it planted
in [my] soul two permanent centers of preoccupation: the question of varieties of human beings . . . and the question of what
variables of personality are chiefly involved in the production of
dissonant theoretical systems. (Murray, 1968, pp. 288–89)

During Easter vacation of the year Murray spent at Cambridge University, he was able to spend three weeks of daily
sessions and long weekends with Jung in Zurich, "from which
explosive experience . . . he emerged a reborn man" (Murray,
1968, p. 287). From Jung, Murray learned to understand his
stuttering problem and its relationship to the psychological effects of the lateral strabismus. But Jung's impact went far be-

yond the merely personal, as is clear from Murray's ecstatic description:

> This was my first opportunity to weigh psychoanalysis in a balance; and I recommend it as one method of measuring the worth of any brand of psychology. Take your mysteries, your knottiest dilemmas, to a fit exponent of a system and judge the latter by its power to order and illuminate your whole being. . . . I had no scales to weigh out Dr. Jung, the first full-blooded, spherical— and Goethian, I should say—intelligence I had ever met, the man whom the judicious Prinzhorn called "the ripest fruit on the tree of psychoanalytic knowledge." We talked for hours, sailing down the lake and smoking before the hearth of his Faustian retreat. "The great floodgates of the wonder-world swung open," and I saw things that my philosophy had never dreamt of. Within a month a score of bi-horned problems were resolved, and I went off decided on depth psychology. I had *experienced* the unconscious, something not to be drawn out of books. (Murray, 1940, p. 153)

It can truly be said that Murray's encounter with Jung qualifies as "a gratuitous answer to an unspoken prayer" (Murray, 1968, p. 289).

From that time on, all of the threads of Murray's experience that did not find adequate expression in surgery began to fall into place, pushing him inexorably toward psychology. In addition to the already mentioned influences, there was also art, a subject matter surprisingly late to have an impact on him. Murray had been reading "a galaxy of seminal books, especially the work of Nietzsche, Dostoevski, Tolstoy, Proust, and Hardy" (Murray, 1968, p. 291). Also exerting a strong humanistic pull were the music of Beethoven, Wagner, and Puccini, the poetry of E. A. Robinson, and the plays of Eugene O'Neill. Murray met the latter two artists and a number of other poets and dramatists, and attended rehearsals of plays. He dabbled in art himself. In short, in many, many personal ways, the path toward psychology was traversed all the while surgery seemed to be his profession.

It now appears somewhat less surprising that Morton Prince should have offered to take Murray as his assistant in founding a clinic at Harvard College. This clinic, which may well have been the first specializing in psychological matters outside of a medical school, was to be devoted to research into the nature of personality and only secondarily to service to the community. Suddenly, Murray was to have his chance to do research on personality and call it his work. So, when the man who had been an incurable stutterer for 24 years, who had an aversion to public speaking, and who had never had a formal psychology course, accepted an instructorship in psychology, it seemed to him like a wonderful "instance of chance and the prepared mind" (Murray, 1968, p. 291).

As in Allport's case, the forces leading Murray to psychology also provided a basis for swift rejection of the behavioristic, reductionistic emphasis then current in the field, and an embracing of more humanistic approaches. But Allport rejected the very depth psychology that the young Murray found so valuable. To Allport, psychoanalysis seemed an instrument for degrading and manipulating man, by focusing on the unconscious and infantile bases of behavior. Murray chose to emphasize the very opposite implications of depth psychology; namely, that through scrutiny of one's unconscious, new and greater control over one's behavior could be achieved: By making the unconscious conscious, one gains the power to take all of oneself into account in planning a life. Perhaps the difference between Murray and Allport is Murray's significant and troublesome behaviors (for example, stuttering) over which he could not exercise control, and his finding out, through Jung, that control could be achieved through scrutiny of the psyche in depth. From the beginning, Allport's life seems to have been well-ordered and sufficiently free of such obtrusive signs of difficulty that his meeting with Freud could turn him off rather than on. Of course, we are not here discussing which man was right, but rather how the intellectual experiences of the past form themselves into conceptual and ideological convictions.

Murray dismissed psychological behaviorism summarily, in a manner similar to Allport, but different from Maslow. Whereas Allport's basis for dismissing psychological behaviorism was ideological, Murray's was more informal, personal, and emotional, at least at first. It is surprising, therefore, that Murray did not go through a period of entertaining behaviorism before rejecting it, as did Maslow, who also had little formal basis for an immediate rejection. But it must be recalled that Murray never studied psychology in school, whereas Maslow did. In a sense, Murray had nothing to entertain, for though the dominant trend in American psychology was behavioristic, he did not have to encounter it. Also, it must be remembered that Murray did pursue a career in surgery at first. Perhaps this represented for him an entertaining of cold, manipulative, nonintimate approaches to living, and perhaps this entertainment was prepared and fostered by his conservative, upper-class family background. In some ways, then, Murray's eventual choice of psychology represented a detachment from childhood influences.

Professional Maturity

With the assumption of academic posts, Allport, Maslow, and Murray entered into their intellectual and professional maturity. To be sure, there will be value in continuing to consider the influences upon them effected by colleagues, friends, and social events. But from this point on, it is essential to also consider the manner and extent to which they influenced the people and institutions with which they had contact.

Allport's first appointment at Harvard in 1924 was, you will recall, in social ethics. The chairman of that department was Richard Cabot, the Boston Brahmin. This man, simultaneously a cardiologist, ethical philosopher, and philanthropist, had a deep effect on young Allport. Cabot's excellence, integrity, and commitments were much what Allport would have valued for himself. In 1936, because Cabot believed in him enough to offer financial support, Allport was able to take a semester off to complete his famous personality book (Allport, 1968b, p. 389). Cabot operated a trust to support worthy scholars, and Allport was made a trustee. After Cabot's death, Allport assumed a directorship in another of his projects, the Cambridge-Somerville Youth Study, which continues to this day as an invaluable source of research data.

Several other colleague-friends influenced Allport during this early professional period. Chief among them were Edwin G. Boring, in whose introductory psychology course the eager, conscientious Allport asked to assist. This relationship blossomed later when Boring was chairman of the Department of Psychology. Allport was also fortunate enough to assist William McDougall in his introductory course. Soon the Department of Social Ethics gave way to the Department of Sociology, headed by Pitirim A. Sorokin, who also had a strong influence on Allport. What Allport seems to have admired most about this group of professionals senior to himself was "a fierce personal and professional integrity . . . powerful erudition and blazing conviction" (Allport, 1968b, p. 391). He felt that he drew much encouragement from their example in pursuing his own ideas in the face of—initially at least—considerable opposition.

Among Allport's contemporaries, he singles out two in particular for mention. One is Henry Murray, who "has been my amiable and supportive colleague. . . . Our fields of interest lie so close together that by unspoken agreement we allow a 'narcissism of slight differences' to keep us in a state of friendly separation. . . . I derive from Murray a great deal of stimulation and encouragement" (Allport, 1968b, p. 391). The other influential contemporary was Peter A. Bertocci, a philosopher who supported Allport in self-theory and wanted to push him to an even greater emphasis on volition than Allport felt was natural for him.

Allport left Harvard in 1926 to teach psychology at Dartmouth for four years. This was a more relaxed environment, permitting him time to reflect once again on the structure of personality and to begin plans for the textbook on that topic he was to publish later. When McDougall left Harvard, Boring offered Allport the vacant position in social psychology. Having long since developed a deep attachment to his alma mater, Allport accepted the job and returned to Cambridge in 1930. He was followed there to pursue graduate studies by some of his Dartmouth undergraduates, including Hadley Cantril, Henry Odbert, and Leonard Doob.

The bulk of Allport's time in the many years spent at Harvard was devoted to personality and social psychology. With Vernon, he produced a book on expressive movement (Allport and Vernon, 1953) and a questionnaire to measure the relative importance of Spranger's six values (Allport and Vernon, 1933). There were in those years many collaborations with students, including Postman, Bruner, Thomas Pettigrew, and Gardner Lindzey, as well as those students who had followed from Dartmouth.

Allport also assumed responsibilities to his profession beyond those performed at Harvard. He was on various committees, and edited the influential *Journal of Abnormal and Social Psychology* for a period of years. At Harvard, he became chairman of the newly formed Department of Psychology, which had broken away from philosophy. Karl Lashley came to fill one of the three permanencies on the staff, Boring held another, and Allport was appointed to the third. In 1937, in the midst of all this administrative activity, his personality textbook was published. The book had a profound impact on the field, virtually defining for many years what was and was not to be considered important in the study of personality. In the book, Allport

. . . wanted to fashion an experimental science, so far as appropriate, but chiefly I wanted an "image of man" that would allow

us to test in full whatever democratic and humane potentialities
that he might possess. I did not think of man as innately "good,"
but I was convinced that by and large American psychology gave
man less than his due by depicting him as a bundle of unrelated
reaction tendencies. . . . I regarded my own approach as being
in the tradition of academic psychology, and I felt that my emphasis should be on normality rather than on pathology. . . . The
book . . . also reiterated the challenge that any adequate psychology of personality must deal with the essential uniqueness
of every personal structure. (Allport, 1968b, pp. 194–95)

Allport also began to publish in social psychology at this time
(for example, Allport, 1935; Allport and Cantril, 1934). In
1939, two years after the appearance of the personality textbook, Allport was elected to the presidency of the American
Psychological Association.

World War II wrought quite a change in Allport's activities.
In general, he avoided employment in governmental agencies,
preferring instead to tailor his teaching and educative activities
to the social needs that had emerged. With Henry Murray, he
began a seminar in "morale research" which was to continue
long after the war. A joint manuscript was produced, but never
published. Allport also spent considerable time finding jobs
for the lesser-known intellectual refugees from Hitler-domi-
nated Europe. Out of this work came a manuscript on personality under social catastrophe (Allport, Bruner, and Jandorf, 1941). Allport also wrote a daily syndicated feature in
the *Boston Traveler* which endeavored to counteract and ex-
pose harmful wartime rumors. This led to his offering, with
Postman, a course on race relations for Boston police. A final
outgrowth of this was a book on rumor (Allport and Postman,
1947).

Being at heart a liberal and a social reformer, Allport was
influential in starting the Society for the Psychological Study
of Social Issues in 1936. Functioning as a division of the
American Psychological Association, this society has cham-

pioned many important social causes. Allport once served as its president.

It became apparent that Harvard would have to prepare for a tremendous increase in enrollment as the war drew to a close. This need for expansion was fertile ground for the seeds of change in the Department of Psychology already sown by an apparent rift between those who were biologically oriented and those who were socially oriented. Once again, Allport was influential as a force for change. In 1946, the Department of Social Relations was formed as an entity separate from the Department of Psychology. Allport joined the new unit, and served it as chairman of its Committee on Higher Degrees until close to his death. The new department well expressed Allport's convictions and interests, being comprised of sociologists, social psychologists, clinical psychologists, and cultural anthropologists. The expansion of this department led to valuable associations with such colleagues as George Homans, Jerome Bruner, M. Brewster Smith, Samuel Stouffer, Richard Solomon, Robert White, Talcott Parsons, and, more recently, Roger Brown, David McClelland, and Herbert Kelman.

By the 1950s, Allport was inundated with professional responsibilities and with requests to speak and write for various audiences. He managed for several years more to offer his enormously popular introductory course in Social Relations, but then gave it to younger colleagues. He wrote, spoke, and traveled extensively. In 1953 he was elected president of the Eastern Psychological Association. In 1955, he published *Becoming: Basic Considerations in a Psychology of Personality*, perhaps his most important statement on personality since his original textbook on this topic. He later revised and expanded that textbook (Allport, 1961), and during the same period, published many works on social psychology. Harvard's Departments of Social Relations and Psychology were brought under one roof in 1965 in the impressive William James Hall. Allport writes that it was "a wrench to leave Emerson Hall, which as student and teacher I had inhabited continuously for fifty years (less . . . the interval at Dartmouth)" (Allport, 1968b, p. 404). But by this time, Allport was in semi-retirement.

Allport was appointed the first Richard Clarke Cabot Professor of Social Ethics in 1966. He says:

> Since Dr. Cabot was my first "boss" at Harvard, having much influence upon my career first and last, the appointment seemed to me to complete fittingly an intellectual cycle as well as a cycle of sentiment. (Allport, 1968b, p. 404)

On October 9, 1967, one month before his seventieth birthday, Allport died of lung cancer. He had received virtually every honor the profession can bestow during his career. In addition to the honors already mentioned, he received the gold medal of the American Psychological Foundation in 1963, and the award of the American Psychological Association for distinguished scientific contributions in 1964. Allport left a dozen books and countless articles, forewords, and reviews, in addition to two tests. His interests and energies ranged widely. A generalist of his scope, who is nevertheless careful and scholarly, is not likely to appear again in the near future.

Maslow, too, led a varied and active professional life. After receiving his Ph.D. at the University of Wisconsin, Maslow spent several years there in the capacities of Assistant Instructor in Psychology (1930–34) and Teaching Fellow in Psychology (1934–35). He then became a Carnegie Fellow at Columbia University, staying from 1935 through 1937. Maslow next served as Associate Professor at Brooklyn College until 1951. From 1947 to 1949, he was plant manager at the Maslow Cooperage Corporation, an organization conceived and organized by Maslow and his brothers. Maslow was professor and chairman of the Department of Psychology at Brandeis University from 1951 until shortly before his death.

Taking a leave of absence from Brandeis in March of 1969, Maslow accepted the first four-year grant from the W. P.

Laughlin Foundation. He intended to study the philosophy of democratic politics, economics, and ethics generated by humanistic psychology, because he was greatly concerned at the current loss of faith in American values. More specifically, he intended to pull together relevant thoughts in a new book. But in the spring of 1970, he died of a heart attack after a history of heart disease, at the age of 62.

Maslow, like Allport, was deeply involved in his profession and was profusely honored by it. He served on the council of the Society for Psychological Study of Social Issues, was a member of Phi Beta Kappa and Sigma Xi, and was a fellow of the New York Academy of Sciences and of several divisions of the American Psychological Association. Maslow was also president of the Massachusetts State Psychological Association, of the Divisions of Personality and Social Psychology and of Esthetics (of the American Psychological Association), and of the American Psychological Association itself.

Maslow shifted from studying animals to studying humans following his graduate student days at Wisconsin, but the content of his interests persisted. His doctoral dissertation had been an observational study of sexual behavior in monkeys. Later, his interest transferred to interview studies of sex and love in humans. Maslow felt that the dominance of male monkeys in sexual behavior was "strongly related to the fantasies and adaptations of humans" (Maslow, 1968c, p. 37).

> The relationship between man's impulses to self-esteem and his sexual feelings and attitudes became apparent, as well as the sexual consequences of feeling uncertain about one's masculinity or femininity. . . . a man can become a homosexual. Or he may compensate and become a Don Juan. It works the same way for women. Or a woman might well become frigid. (Maslow, 1968c, p. 54)

Maslow's studies of sex continued until the start of World War II. He felt these studies provided a considerable basis for improving the quality of life:

I thought that working on sex was the easiest way to help mankind. If I could discover a way to improve the sexual life of even
one per cent, then I could improve the whole species. (Maslow,
1968c, p. 54)

Most of Maslow's sex studies considerably predated Kinsey's
work. Maslow was distinctly unsatisfied with the noted sexolo-
gist's approach, finding it unnecessarily cold and derogatory
toward human sexuality. In contrast, Maslow's approach was
warm and appreciative, and inextricably mixed with his ecstasy
over life and his zeal to improve it:

I was fascinated with my research. But I gave up [interviewing]
men. They were useless because they boasted and lied.

I planned one big research project with prostitutes. I thought
we could learn a lot about men from them. . . . The research
never came off. My best interviews were with dear, good, bright
women. I admire women and frankly envy them a bit for the
things I am not. Of course, I feel they should envy me for the
things they are not. . . . If you're doubtful about your masculin-
ity, women are a threat. But women are really kind of perpetual
miracles. They are like flowers, even old ladies. Every person is
a mystery to me, but women are more mysterious to me than
men. So any woman is a fascinating mystery to question for end-
less hours.

I interviewed 120 women with a new form of interview. No
notes; we just talked along until I got some feeling for the personality, then put sex against the background.

Sex has to be considered against love, otherwise it's useless.
What a person does, his overt sexual behavior by itself, is useless.
Behavior is a defense, a way of hiding what you feel, particularly
in regard to sex. The work I did with homosexuals was so revealing; there are lots of secrets there that haven't been touched. If
I were beginning all over again, I'd study homosexuality . . . as
a means to a profound understanding of humanity. (Maslow,
1968c, p. 54)

The early period of Maslow's professional life may be characterized with some accuracy as influenced by the psychoana-

lytic approaches then holding sway in American personology. When Maslow went to Brooklyn College in 1938, he was working on his book on personality and psychopathology (Maslow and Mittelman, 1941). While this book included an early statement on the hierarchy of needs conceptualization, it dealt with psychopathological states as if they were especially valuable bases upon which to understand human behavior generally. Perhaps this assumption was bolstered by Maslow's own psychoanalysis.

There is no doubt that World War II deeply affected all three of the men we are considering. Maslow literally gave up all his previous studies, finding them insufficiently related to the struggle for human survival that was going on. His deep personal involvement and grief over the war is well documented in his own words:

> I gave up everything I was fascinated with in a selfish way around 1941. I felt I must try to save the world and to prevent these horrible wars and this awful hatred and prejudice.
>
> It happened very suddenly, you know. One day just after Pearl Harbor I was driving home and my car was stopped by a poor, pathetic parade.
>
> Boy Scouts and fat people and old uniforms and a flag and someone playing a flute off-key. . . . As I watched, the tears began to run down my face. I felt we didn't understand—not Hitler, nor the Germans, nor Stalin, nor the communists. We didn't understand any of them. I felt that if we could understand, then we could make progress. I had a vision of a peace table, with people sitting around it, talking about human nature and hatred and war and peace and brotherhood.
>
> I was too old to go into the army. It was at that moment that I realized that the rest of my life must be devoted to discovering a psychology for the peace table.
>
> That moment changed my whole life and determined what I have done since. Since that moment in 1941 I've devoted myself to developing a theory of human nature that could be tested by experiment and research.

I wanted to prove that human beings are capable of something grander than war and prejudice and hatred. I wanted to make science consider all the problems that nonscientists have been handling—religion, poetry, values, philosophy, art.

I went about it by trying to understand great people, the best specimens of mankind I could find. I found that many of them reported having something like mystical experiences. (Maslow, 1968c, pp. 54–55)

In this statement are several important emphases that were to guide the rest of Maslow's professional endeavor. First, it is clear that for him to theorize about personality is to provide a basis for improving it. His is no value-free orientation, based on knowledge for knowledge's sake. In this regard, the war must have congealed and pinpointed the personal sense of human suffering and waste stemming from his childhood years, leaving him with the conclusion that there was simply no time to lose in the matter of human survival. Secondly, and consistent with the emphasis on improving life, is the selection of the best persons to study rather than the worst. Prior to the war, when Maslow was still fairly strongly influenced by psychoanalytic theory, he probably agreed with the assumption that the most fertile insights about mankind are found in the study of pathology. Maslow adopted the opposite view after the war. Finally, the vivid statement quoted above constitutes what Maslow later came to conceptualize as a peak experience—an intense, often mystical experience that radically changes a person in one fell swoop. Apparently, the occurrence of such experiences in Maslow himself served as an impetus to conceptualize them as important in the self-actualizing, transcendent life.

Maslow threw himself into humanistic endeavor from this point on. He construed as allies such psychologists as Allport, Rollo May, Carl Rogers, Warren Bennis, and Chris Argyris. Maslow relates an interesting anecdote about Allport, with whom he was well acquainted:

Gordon [Allport] was very reserved, you know. He was a great psychologist . . . but he was a man who never unbent socially. One afternoon he was standing [in my living room] looking out this window and his face suddenly flushed deep red. "What's the matter?" I asked. "My wife and I courted on that island," he said. (Maslow, 1968c, p. 37)

Maslow nominates Socrates, Plato, Spinoza, Jefferson, and Alfred North Whitehead as his intellectual ancestors. Indeed, when asked how he fortified himself against the attacks of other psychologists, less willing than he to consider values and advocate directions of the good life, Maslow answered:

I have a secret. I talk over the heads of the people in front of me to my own private audience. I talk to people I love and respect. To Socrates and Aristotle and Spinoza and Thomas Jefferson and Abraham Lincoln. And when I write, I write for them. This cuts out a lot of crap. (Maslow, 1968c, p. 56)

Maslow's message is clearly one of love and human sensitivity rather than competition and aggression. He blames technology and modern, complex social structures for a deterioration of life and values.

We've technologized everything, you know—education, work, politics, the social sciences. . . . [People] become fascinated with the machine. It's almost a neurotic love. They're like the man who spends Sunday polishing his car instead of stroking his wife. (Maslow, 1968c, p. 55)

Maslow is in favor of each person fulfilling his potentialities. Presaging the women's liberation movement, Maslow felt this was especially problematical for women because of their role in our society:

I remember I once gave a lecture to a group of women about growing-tip statistics and there were tears and I was kissed. . . . This was a group of bright women who were sure their intelligence scared off men, and always would. I was so excited about the new woman we're developing—the woman who can fulfill herself.

I warned them that if a real woman looks like a pussycat instead of a lioness, she'll attract pussycats—and who wants them. A lioness should attract lions, and she will if she doesn't hide her capability and intelligence. A lion is attracted by the lioness; she heats him up. (Maslow, 1968c, p. 56)

Although Maslow is in favor of women assuming a position of equality with men, this does not mean that he sees men and women as the same. Actually, he clearly distinguished between the natural propensities of the sexes:

All serious men are Messianic. They have no interest in power or money or in anything but their mission. Females are not Messianic. And a man has a sense of duty to this mission. He neglects his health, risks his life, subordinates all else to his Messianic vision.

Man's duty is to the three books he has to write before he dies. A woman's commitment is to her man, and to her cubs . . . a woman . . . can love one child more intensely than I can, but I can love one million children more intensely. I can write a book or devote my energies for the sake of one million kids whom I've never seen. And that's a really profound male–female difference—at least in our culture. (Maslow 1968c, p. 56)

Whether or not this position is justified, it is not likely to endear Maslow to the women's liberation movement as much as the prior quoted position!

Clearly, one influence leading Maslow to develop the theory of self-actualization was World War II. The war was a marker of the baseness to which man could stoop. But Maslow also had personal experiences that showed the heights to which man could reach. Two mentors and friends in particular were enormously influential. To young Maslow, fresh from graduate school and the Midwest, Ruth Benedict and Max Wertheimer seemed like Gods when he encountered them in New York City. In Maslow's flowing account of their importance to him, one can see operating the experiences that must have kept him from being soured by World War II:

My investigations on self-actualization were not planned to be research and did not start out as research. They started out as the effort of a young intellectual to try to understand two of his teachers whom he loved, adored, and admired and who were very, very wonderful people. It was a kind of high-IQ devotion. I could not be content simply to adore, but sought to understand why these two people were so different from the run-of-the-mill people in the world. These two people were Ruth Benedict and Max Wertheimer. They were my teachers after I came with a Ph.D. from the West to New York City, and they were not quite people but something more than people. My own investigation began as a prescientific or nonscientific activity. I made descriptions and notes on Max Wertheimer, and I made notes on Ruth Benedict. When I tried to understand them, think about them, and write about them in my journal and my notes, I realized in one wonderful moment that their two patterns could be generalized. I was talking about a kind of person, not about two noncomparable individuals. There was wonderful excitement in that. I tried to see whether this pattern could be found elsewhere, and I did find it elsewhere, in one person after another. (Maslow, 1968c, p. 57)

This vivid picture of the greatness in man, superimposed upon a background of his meanness (as in war) is reminiscent of Maslow's earlier experience, in which there was a sharp discrepancy between his social ostracism and the nurturance he received from a few revered teachers.

In the last years of his life Maslow became a popular leader of the humanistic movement both inside and outside of psychology. People from every walk of life knew him because of his preaching of the humanistic doctrine, and especially because of his association with and support of the sensitivity group phenomenon. Actually, he helped launch this phenomenon, giving heavy support to Esalen Institute from its earliest days. It will come as no surprise that Maslow was completely impervious to criticisms of him for his "soft-headedness" with regard to sensitivity training. To him, anything that helped people to love each other more and to experience life richly could not be bad, whatever the role of faddishness in it. He valued attempts more than he feared errors. He could not understand a discouraging attitude toward sensitivity training at a time when American life seemed so corrupted by technology, bureaucracy, hypocrisy, materialism, aggression, and war. Until the time of his death, he was active in the American Humanistic Society.

As a man, Maslow was emotional, warm, given to tremendous enthusiasms, generous almost to a fault. He was less scholarly and perhaps less rigorous than Allport. Allport, too, felt the need to try to provide a basis in the study of personality for the improvement of living. But Maslow's was a more passionate nature, steeped in early suffering and tempered by need. The need in him to serve society assumed the proportions of a personal crusade, a life-and-death struggle. The books he wrote after World War II were both humanistic and Messianic. Allport was no less committed to social service, but certainly more restrained and careful. Maslow was the more appropriate man to lead popular movements.

To take up the thread of Murray's intellectual development, you will recall that he was the unconventional choice of Morton Prince to assist in the Psychological Clinic at Harvard. This clinic was dedicated to research into personality and psychopathology. Its existence outside of a medical school—in the liberal arts and sciences wing of the university—was of critical importance, for the freedom from pressure allowed the clinic to be of service in a practical sense. Murray became assistant professor and director of the clinic in 1928, a role for which Prince had groomed him. His connection with this institution was to guide and determine his entire professional career. His role there permitted him to express his deep and abiding zeal for personological research, and facilitated his bringing together an extraordinary set of colleagues. On the basis of his work in the clinic, Murray was made an associate professor in 1937.

During those years, the Harvard clinic's orientation was heavily psychoanalytic; it was one of the few institutions where Freud's thinking was being put to a systematic empirical test. From the beginning, however, Murray's interest was primarily in normal rather than abnormal people. The extension of psychoanalytic thinking into normality seemed natural to him, as he had come to believe in the indispensability of the concept of unconscious processes in explaining behavior. His interest in psychoanalytic theory also led in other directions:

> Believing in addition (against the sturdy opposition of Dr. Prince) that Freud's theoretical system was more applicable than any other to an understanding of dysfunctionings, [I] became one of the founders of the Boston Psychoanalytic Society, went through the then-existing course of formal Freudian training, including an analysis by Dr. Franz [Hans] Sachs, and for a number of years practiced orthodox psychoanalysis, modified by ideas derived from Jung, Adler, and Rank. These were the activities which incurred the disapproval of Karl Lashley and through him of President Conant, whose inclination to fire [me] was eventually overruled by various considerations advanced by Gordon Allport, Whitehead, and several other brave supporters. (Murray, 1968, p. 292)

From time to time, all three of our theorists have incurred the displeasure of powerful exponents of traditional academic psychology, which at the time was largely behavioristic and psychophysical. But Murray's difficulties were very direct, involving a considerable threat to his job. It is interesting to note that Allport came to the aid of his fellow personologist, even though they must by then have disagreed sharply over the value of psychoanalysis.

Murray's difficulties with department members did not end here. As he became more and more concerned with understanding normal behavior, psychoanalytic thought seemed limited because of its emphasis on pathology. Murray began to develop the concept of need, so basic to his mature thought. This kind of thinking received a very cold reception, coming at a time

when McDougall's emphasis on instincts had been dethroned
by Watson, who emphasized a strict adherence to observables
alone. Questions of consciousness and purpose were regarded
as naive by Murray's colleagues. As did Allport and Maslow,
Murray reached to legendary great men for support rather
than to immediate colleagues:

> William James (who was said by a later member of the Harvard
> department to have done unparalleled harm to psychology) had
> become one of [my] major exemplars by that time, and [I found
> myself] agreeing with almost everything [this] hero had to say—
> completely, for example, with the heretical statement that "Indi-
> viduality is founded in feeling; and the recesses of feeling, the
> darker, blinder strata of character, are the only places in the
> world in which we catch real fact in the making, and directly
> perceive how events happen and how work is actually done."
> (Murray, 1968, p. 293)

Whereas Allport and Maslow had made their primary commitment to the academic departments in which they taught,
Murray's energies were spent primarily in the Harvard clinic
and in his psychotherapy practice. His tie with Harvard was
less solidly academic, though he did do some lecturing.
Whereas the heresies of Allport and Maslow could be margin-
ally tolerated, therefore, those of Murray branded him as a
dangerous eccentric. This role of eccentric must have fit Murray easily because of his early life and his sojourn in medicine.
Interestingly enough, he has detailed the grounds upon which
he felt little or no concern about being rejected by his peers.
It should be noted that the rejection was real and was more extreme than was the case for Allport or Maslow. For example,
Murray was not granted tenure at Harvard until he was 55
years of age!

Murray found that several factors permitted him to maintain his heretical views:

> (1) Having been trained in a more exact science, [I] did not
> feel compelled for the sake of self-esteem to put exemplary
> technical competence in a less exact science at the top of [my]

hierarchy of aims. (2) [I] had come to psychology with the hope of advancing current knowledge about human beings, not to raise [my] status on the totem pole of scientists. (3) There was nothing original about [my] ideas: they were derived from a score of world-famous medical psychologists whose practical aims had kept them far closer to the raw facts than occupants of the groves of academe had ever got. (4) [My] varied, intimate relations with hospital patients . . . together with privately-experienced emotional revolutions, upsurges from below consciousness, had given [me] a sense of functional fitness, the feeling that all parts of [my] self were in unison with [my] professional identity . . . and that [I] was more advantaged in these ways than were many of the book-made academics who talked as if they had lost contact with the springs of their own natures. (5) Despite [my] obnoxious behavior now and then, the permanent members of the department, Professor Boring and Professor Pratt, were invariably friendly, helpful, and indulgent. . . . (6) [I] was not much of a teacher, but because of the drawing power of psychoanalysis [I] was reinforced from the beginning . . . by having a number of promising graduate students—such as Donald Mac-Kinnon, Saul Rosenzweig, Nevitt Sanford . . . and Robert White. . . . (7) [I] was not tempted to toe the line or be rewarded theories and experiments, as some others were, by economic need or even by any continuing, unrealistic want for recognition from the elite of [my] profession. (Murray, 1968, p. 294)

The years Murray spent at Harvard were particularly rich and fruitful years in the life of the clinic, however much opposition there may have been in the department. Murray and the students mentioned above stimulated each other tremendously in their massive study of fifty normal Harvard students. The results of this study, which used every conceivable kind of measurement to get at personality, were published in the famous *Explorations in Personality* (Murray, 1938). Just prior to that, Murray published the equally famous *Thematic Apperception Test* (Murray and Morgan, 1935). His collaborator on this, Christiana Morgan, a woman deeply influenced by

Jung, was to become a lifelong colleague. After editing the manuscript of *Explorations in Personality,* Murray left for an official absence from the clinic that was to span nine of the succeeding eleven years. In part, this absence was a vacation with his wife and daughter, during which they visited Jung in Switzerland, observed the frenzy of Hitler's Germany with fear, and finally "spent a memorable evening with Dr. and Anna Freud in the room where that astounding corpus of cultural history had been shaped" (Murray, 1968, p. 305).

Murray returned to the Harvard clinic, which had been directed in his absence by Robert White, in 1941. There an extraordinary group had gathered to engage once again in the multiform approach to personality assessment that had been pioneered by Murray. Among those there were Leo Bellak, Silvan Tomkins, Frederick Wyatt, Robert Holt, and Morris Stein. But the enthusiastic, brave beginning they made was nipped in the bud by the beginning of World War II. One of the publications that did manage to get finished was *A Clinical Study of Sentiments* (Murray and Morgan, 1945), in which an emphasis on values was added to that on needs.

Murray left Harvard in 1943, with the rank of major in the Army Medical Corps (subsequently lieutenant colonel). Together with other former collaborators, such as MacKinnon, Stein, and James Miller, Murray established and directed an assessment service for the Office of Strategic Services. This group screened candidates for complex, secret, and dangerous missions. By the time this task was done, a remarkable number of important contemporary personologists, such as Tomkins, Fiske, Heine, and the others already mentioned, had participated. For his work, Murray was awarded the Legion of Merit in 1946. The activities of this group were published in *Assessment of Men* (Murray, 1948).

Murray returned to Harvard in 1947 as a part-time lecturer in clinical psychology in the newly formed Department of Social Relations. He established the Psychological Clinic Annex in 1949, where he and several students, including Gardner

Lindzey, Edward Shneidman, and Gerhard Nielsen, continued studies as before. In 1950, he became professor, and in 1962, professor emeritus.

The tragic events of World War II had persuaded Murray of the necessity of expanding his personological frame of reference to embrace social systems and cultural determinants of behavior. His sophistication in these extensions was deepened through friendships with Clyde Kluckhohn and Talcott Parsons. The entire thrust of these late theoretical ruminations was to find a viable alternative to war.

> The OSS assessment job had taken [me] around the world to check up on the errors they had made, and [I] happened to be in Kunming, testing officer candidates for the Chinese Nationalist Army, when the news of Hiroshima, announced over the radio of [my] jeep, set off a hectic procession of horrendous images of the world's fate, which ever since have magnetically directed the path of countless currents of imagination toward some far-off ultimate solution, in the constant view of which, year by year and month by month, short-range international strategies and tactics could be more creatively designed. While others were thinking of ways of reducing momentary tensions and quieting the anxieties of their fellow citizens, [I] was oriented toward the total abolition of war. Peace must be insured by a world government of an unprecedented type, which would never be established or never last without a radical transformation of ethnocentric sentiments and values on both sides of our divided world; and a transformation of this nature would never occur without some degree of synthesis of the best features of the two opposing cultural systems; and this would not take place creatively except in sight of an unprecedented vision and conception of world relationship and fellowship, a kind of superordinate natural religion, or mythological philosophy. (Murray, 1968, pp. 306–307)

Much of Murray's work to find an alternative to war exists at this point only in notes. In 1962, the same year of his retirement, Murray had to face "the sudden death of [my] superlatively good and loyal wife, . . . and . . . the fading of the mental

energies on which [I] had been counting to deal with one or two
at least of the ten half-finished books that are calling for completion . . ." (Murray, 1968, p. 307). But this is hardly the
end of the story. Murray remarried in 1969, and continues hard
at work. He, like Allport, was perturbed by the move from
his Psychological Clinic Annex to the new William James Hall,
and spends most of his time now working at his home nearby.
It is fitting that this man, who was so ostracized once, and yet
who influenced an entire field and several generations of personologists, should have been honored by receiving the Distinguished Scientific Contribution Award of the American Psychological Association as well as the Gold Medal Award of the
American Psychological Foundation.

Unlike Maslow, Murray has never been a joiner or leader of
social movements. Murray has believed in and worked for a
set of humanistic values, and has drawn together around him
like-minded colleagues for mutual stimulation and accomplishment, but he has been aloof from popular movements *per se*.
He has never in his commitment to the improvement of life—
unlike Allport—worked primarily through an endorsement of,
and solid membership in, the existing establishment. In contrast to the other two personologists, Murray emerges as more
of an isolate, though no less dedicated to studying, understanding, and changing personality and the social system. In his own,
separate way, Murray has had an enormous influence on personology; his research and theorizing have virtually shaped
methodological and substantive usage in this field for many
years. His early emphasis on psychoanalytic thought occurred
because this seemed humanistic in contrast to American behaviorism. His later emphasis on normality and need analysis
represents an attempt to be even more humanistic than psychoanalysis permits.

Concluding Remarks

Clearly, the general orientations toward personality theorizing that were discussed in Chapter One, and on which Allport,

Maslow, and Murray agree, are generalizations of personal commitments prepared for in early life and solidified in adulthood. But the events in each theorist's life which influenced these general attitudinal agreements were not always greatly similar. In this sense, these three men well exemplify the personologist's belief that the explanation of behavior cannot be fully convincing if it deals solely and simplistically with the social forces impinging upon individuals. In social terms, the lives of Allport, Maslow, and Murray differed radically. Maslow was a product of the lower class, in both economic and educational senses. It is true that in both those senses he himself rose rapidly from humble beginnings—happily enough, his parents had emigrated to the socially mobile United States—but the marks of early ostracism and suffering remained. More than the other two theorists, Maslow was concerned about the evil in men, and insistent on changing it to good. Allport was an almost prototypical example of the Midwestern Protestant middle class. He grew up with an unshakable belief in man's goodness and in the importance of a life of public service. He identified with the establishment—seeing it as a force for valuable social stability and orderly change—much more than did Maslow. And Murray is an aristocrat—a product of the Eastern, sophisticated upper classes. He sees man's potentialities for both good and evil, and, of course, wants to help actualize the good. But there is not in this the stridency lent by early personal suffering at the hands of others. Nor is there the unquestioned assumption that the good will win out or is somehow stronger than the evil. This relative detachment is also exemplified in Murray's aloofness from the establishment and from popular movements as means of effecting change, or, for that matter, insuring stability.

In spite of general attitudinal differences, which seem to follow so directly from the social class differences marking their lives, Allport, Maslow, and Murray do agree on many things. Their agreements—which can well be summarized as a humanistic stance—were presented in Chapter One as conceptualizations of man as proactive, psychologically organized, complex, rational, unique, and future oriented. From early age on into maturity, all three theorists were different from their peers (uniqueness) and seem to have relied upon verbal and mental facility (rationality). They all seem to have outgrown the most direct early parental influences—though important influences they were—and achieved an orientation toward life in which they shaped their own experiences (proactive), rejecting some social pressures and accepting others in a manner reflecting judgment (rationality). Each in his own way changed a lot in terms of the specifics of commitments and behaviors (complexity), all the while progressing toward greater actualization of the goals they pinpointed and solidified by the time they became adult (future orientation). Truly, it would be difficult to understand the full meaning of many specific episodes and decisions in their lives without a knowledge of the rest (psychological organization, or holism). If generalization from one's own experience is a sound basis for developing a set of beliefs about personality, then a humanistic stance, a concern with helping mankind achieve a creative, cooperative, peaceful way of life, is so obviously stamped on the personal lives of Allport, Maslow, and Murray as to need no further comment.

It is difficult to discern personal life influences on the actual concepts or formal theorizing of Allport, Maslow, and Murray. Nonetheless, it is possible to trace some basic decisions concerning the main thrust of formal theorizing to personal struggles in these prominent psychologists. In a way, the key to Allport's formal theorizing is carried in the concept of functional autonomy, underlying as it does the distinction between propriate and opportunistic functioning. One may start life by performing on demand, for the rewards granted by others and to avoid punishment from them, but one does not end there, Allport feels. Even performing in this initially conventional way leads to changes in the direction of more personal, idiosyncratic commitments. The conventional or conformist conscience of childhood is replaced by the generic, personal set of values marking maturity. Performing to please others gives way to performing to please oneself. This emphasis on turning initially imposed values and commitments into some personally satisfying versions comes rather directly out of a concern in Allport's own life. Social service, intellectualism, and hard work were values imposed by his father and mother. As Allport matured, he could not and did not wish to break these commitments, but struggled to develop versions of them more suited to his own interests, experiences, and capabilities. He tried to serve society by teaching ethics, not by running a hospital. Hard work and intellectualism were values pursued in his own way, by being a scholar, scientist, and psychologist— ways that his parents may barely have imagined for him.

A main thrust of Maslow's formal theorizing is the hierarchy of needs, which conceptualizes man as determined in his concerns by his history of satisfaction. If biological needs are unsatisfied, they will be paramount, but, once satisfied, they give ground to social needs. If the social needs are unsatisfied, they help type the person, but if they are satisfied, then psychological needs emerge. The psychological needs are the quintessential concerns of man, but are not always reached. It is not surprising that such a conceptualization would be formulated by the small, poor son of immigrant parents, imbued with ambition to better himself. As a youngster, Maslow was not always sure where his next meal was coming from. He indicates having felt socially ostracized. Biological and social concerns may well have dominated his early life, and been of considerable importance to his parents as well. But through fortunate encounters with nurturant, supportive teachers and with his wife-to-be, Maslow may well have experienced a shift from these basic concerns to more intellectual ones. It seems plausible that there is a strong personal basis in this struggle for "a place in the sun," for formulating the hierarchy of needs as a universal.

If one steps back from Murray's theorizing to find some way

of characterizing it, one is likely to come up with the extra-ordinary diversity and complexity of his view of human be-havior, as expressed formally in the long list of needs and types of needs. There is relatively little concern with how these needs are organized. What seems important is that so many of them can and do exist. In the preceding pages, ample evidence has been given of the extraordinary richness and diversity of Mur-ray's early experience as an upper class New Yorker growing up in the middle of Manhattan Island. In addition, Murray changed his work commitment fairly radically several times in an attempt to find the best way of expressing and coping with the many, sometimes competitive interests and talents he felt. It is only understandable, with such a personal struggle, that he would have stressed in his formal theorizing the complexity and diversity of human needs.

Undoubtedly many other examples of how personal experi-ences influenced the formal theorizing of Allport, Maslow, and Murray could be stated. We have focused only on some of the more obvious and pervasive examples from the lives of these three fascinating men.

Conclusions

Our consideration of the positions of Allport, Maslow, and Murray is now over except for the summarizing. As the positions have been separated into their component parts for purposes of presentation and scrutiny, it would be well to summarize them by putting the parts back together where they belong. The theorists would like that, especially with their holistic emphasis.

Allport presented a theory of personality in which the normal person goes through a brief early period in which his biological animal nature dictates his behavior, but soon emerges into a life guided by the attempt to fulfill his sense of self or proprium. The transition to propriate functioning occurs naturally, as long as it is not blocked by an environment that is too punitive and depriving to satisfactorily satiate the biological needs. Through what is probably the interaction between propriate functioning and the contents and constraints of the environment in which the person lives, he will come to develop some personal dispositions, or structured, organized ways of perceiving, thinking, and acting. Personal dispositions describe the uniqueness of each person, and may be classified only on the basis of generality, not content. To classify on the basis of content denotes that personal dispositions are shared from person to person, a position that is too nomothetic for

161

Allport. In order from most to least general, personal dispositions, according to Allport, may be classified as cardinal (or
genotypic), central (or phenotypic), and secondar.

In Maslow's theory of personality, a person comes into life
possessed of both lower (animalistic) and higher (human)
needs. Maslow, like Allport, believes that the lower needs must
be satisfied before the higher ones can be vigorously expressed.
If the lower, mainly biological, needs are met by an environment that is reasonably nurturant and permissive, then the
higher needs will naturally become the most important. The
higher needs refer to self-actualization, by which Maslow refers not only to a subjective sense of self (as does Allport) but
also to some assumed set of inherent potentialities. Maslow
and Allport agree that it is the interaction of need-determined
behavior and the contents and constraints of the person's environment that determine the style of his life. Maslow is not
so insistent on the view that each person is completely unique;
hence, he theorizes about the major styles of life, or complexes,
that are possible. Presumably, there is one or a set of complexes possible for each level on the hierarchy of needs, Maslow believes. This hierarchy includes, as lower needs, those for
physiological survival, safety, belongingness, and esteem, and
as higher needs, those for self-actualization and cognitive understanding.

In Murray's theory of personality, a person comes into the
world possessing an id, which includes not only antisocial but
also acceptable needs (for example, achievement, sex, power,
affiliation). The requirements of satisfying needs in a complex world precipitates the development of the ego, which includes a wide range of cognitive and action skills. Because
some of the needs expressed by a person violate the taboos
and sanctions of parents and society, a person also develops
a superego, which rides herd on the id and forces the person
to be a responsible member of the collective. To Murray, as
is true also to Allport and Maslow, it is the interaction of the

id (aided by the ego) and society (aided by the superego) that determines the general style of life that develops. Displaying his psychoanalytic allegiance, Murray considers the major complexes of life to be claustral, oral, anal, phallic, and something like mature. These complexes are presumably constituted of particular needs, formed in the period of development in which the activities and conflicts summarized in the names of the complexes are most important.

Inevitably, one simplifies and tidies up in order to offer brief, holistic summaries of theories. The only claim we make for the summaries just presented is that they disclose some general agreements among Allport, Maslow, and Murray without distorting their positions all out of shape. The most striking agreements between the three men are in the form of theorizing. All three theorists assume some inborn, universal set of characteristics that provide the intial thrust for behavior—that get the person going, so to speak. All three also assume that it is the interaction between this thrust and environmental circumstance that determines the person's life style, be it mature or immature. Allport, Maslow, and Murray also recognize the value of conceptualizing some relatively concrete characteristics of personality with which to be able to describe what the person is like (though Allport would not offer lists of such characteristics because of a morphogenic emphasis).

In terms of content, there are striking similarities among Allport's and Maslow's theories. Both make the distinction between animalistic, biological needs on the one hand and humanistic, spiritual needs on the other hand. Both define maturity in terms of the ascendency of the humanistic orientation. Both cast society in the role of that which is a potential hindrance to humanistic development. In these ways, Allport and Maslow fulfill the humanistic emphasis of their metatheoretical stance.

Murray's theory is more complex to analyse. Although he is metatheoretically humanistic, his actual theory still shows

significant signs of psychoanalytic influence. But the changes
he has brought on the psychoanalytic model are all in the humanistic direction. Thus, the id includes socially useful as well
as antisocial motivations. The ego is not merely mediator between id and superego, but has a life of its own. Sometimes
the id functions to decrease conflict by the employment of
defenses; at other times it teams up with the socially useful
motivations, leading to valuable and defense-free activity. And
the superego is not merely the static implant of a particular,
accidentally selected set of parents, but continues to develop
throughout life, becoming more and more selective, sophisticated, and tailored to the person's goals and experience. As
implied in this theory, development is not seen to stop with
puberty, but continues to develop throughout life. The criteria
of maturity that Murray considers possible for people to reach
appears not too dissimilar to the theories assumed by Allport
and Maslow. Remember that Murray's emphasis upon needs
as a basis for understanding the human being has always been
greater than his emphasis on the more psychoanalytic concepts of id, ego, and superego. All things considered, Murray
has gone as far toward humanism as it is possible to go within
a psychoanalytic framework without completely destroying it.
Murray is willing to consider the transcendent, valourous aspects of human functioning but, unlike Allport and Maslow,
does not believe that there is nothing less than heroic in the
normal person.

Not only the metatheories but also the theories of Allport,
Murray, and Maslow show ample emphasis on humanistic
commitment. What remains to be done is to judge the theories
as to their usability. Clearly, none of the three theories has yet
achieved adequate usability. For the most part, the major reasons for this lack have been indicated at the points of their
greatest relevance. The more and less general concepts included in each theory need to be further delineated and unified. A particularly important aspect of this need is for com-

plete operational definition of the less general concepts. Among other things, this would require more explication of the *concrete observables* to which the theories are meant to pertain. Although Murray has attempted some operational definition and data specification, he has hardly carried his attempts far enough, and Allport and Maslow have done even less along these lines. Still another great obstacle to usability is the frequent lack of specification of the relationships between the more and less general concepts and within each of these classes. When some statement concerning relationship is made, it is too likely, especially in Murray's and Maslow's writings, to be couched in very figurative language. This difficulty is particularly apparent in the portions of Murray's theory that come most directly from the psychoanalytic tradition.

Such shortcomings lead even friendly critics to see the theories of Allport, Maslow, and Murray, at this stage in their development, as relegated to post-hoc explanation and to general stimulus value for other psychologists. Significantly, there has not been a great deal of research designed specifically to test concrete predictions generated from the theories. The research that has been relevant to the viewpoints of our three theorists has sprung as much from the humanistic metatheory they share as from their actual theories.

One frequent criticism of these three psychologists does not seem warranted. It is sometimes said that the viewpoints of Allport, Maslow, and Murray are not theories at all, but simply elaborate descriptions of observed facts. Presumably, there is no reference here to shortcomings in usability, except insofar as these contribute to the general frustration of the would-be user, disposing him to adopt a critical orientation. More likely it is the common sense content of many of the concepts that is objectionable. What seems to be overlooked is that the major characteristic of any theoretical concept is generality. For example, if one advanced the concept of courage, and embedded it in a theoretical apparatus that would permit the deduction of particular behaviors in particular contexts, the fact that the behavior might be taken by even an unskilled observer to indicate courage would not make the concept less theoretical. Although the theories of Allport, Maslow, and Murray are not yet at an adequate level of usability, they are genuine theoretical endeavors. It is often the person who has come to identify personality theory with the Freudian approach, strong in its reductionistic orientation, who is unconvinced of the theoretical status of a concept unless it leads to explanations of functioning that contradict his own experience.

There is danger that, in focusing upon limitations and all that remains to be done, the value of what has already been accomplished will be lost from view. Our three theorists have fought hard and persistently for a recognition of the humanistic qualities of man's personality at a time when it was most unfashionable to do so in psychology. If some of the critical remarks made by Allport, Maslow, and Murray seem directed toward outmoded positions, it is largely because of the present accelerating trend toward emphasizing humanistic qualities. This trend must be attributed in no small measure to their influence. The ongoing fight has taken a good deal of time and energy. The careful, rich observation of man's complex, organized, conscious, and changing characteristics, and the continual attempt to describe and generalize what was seen in a meaningful manner, guided throughout by the painful self-consideration called introspection, also has taken a great deal of time. And yet, without these struggles, psychology would not be even as far as it is in attempting to conceptualize the valuable as well as the trying qualities of man. It is now possible, and certainly important, for psychologists to marshal their energies toward increasing the usability of theories such as those of Allport, Maslow, and Murray so that humanistic convictions can be put to empirical tests. This phase of formalization and test can be accomplished. Whatever the eventual outcome, mankind and psychology stand to benefit by an increment in lasting understanding.

Glossary

Abient tendencies. Behavior directed towards avoiding or decreasing a stimulus; can be seen as "tension decreasing." Avoidant behavior (Maslow).

Activity needs. Tendencies to "engage in a certain kind of activity for its own sake. Activity needs are subdivided into *process needs,* involving performance and action from the sheer pleasure to be derived from the exercise of available functions, and *mode needs,* which are satisfied by the excellence of activity rather than its mere occurrence" (Murray, 1954, p. 446).

Actone. A unit of action or behavior. An actone can refer to physical movements, motone, or to a string of words, verbone (Murray).

Adient tendencies. Behavior directed towards increasing and perpetuating stimulation; can be seen as "tension increasing" (Maslow).

Alpha press. A press as it objectively exists (to be distinguished from a *beta press*—the subjective experience of a press). A *press* refers to the effect an outside source has or may have on the individual (Murray, 1938, pp. 115–23).

Alpha situation. A stimulus situation as it exists objectively (to be distinguished from a *beta situation*—the subjective experience of a stimulus situation) (Murray).

Areal factor. A factor derived in a cluster of analysis of expressive behavior, composed of an area of total writing, an area of blackboard figures, and a length of self-rating checks. Motor expansiveness is an important trait involved here (Allport).

Beta press. The subjective experience of a press. *See* Alpha press.

Beta situation. The subjective experience of a stimulus situation. *See* Alpha situation.

Bodily sense. The recognizable experience of one's body. (Allport).

Canalization. The establishment of a stable preference for certain kinds of objects for satisfying needs. *Need*-canalization involves learning which objects are intrinsically proper gratifications and which objects are not. Canalization stands in contrast to the arbitrary associations of classical conditioning. The pattern of canalization helps to define a person's individuality (Maslow, 1954, 138). Originally G. Murphy's concept

Cardinal dispositions. Personal dispositions of great salience, pervasiveness, and consistency which, if they exist in a personality, will set the entire pattern of an individual's life. They are of greater determining magnitude than *secondary dispositions* or *central dispositions* (Allport).

Circular determination. The characteristic of a syndrome referring to "the continual flux of dynamic interaction within a syndrome, whereby any one part is always affected by all other parts, the entire action going on simultaneously" (Maslow, 1954, pp. 37–61). *See* Syndrome.

Claustral complex. Complexes representing residuals of the uterine or prenatal experience. Claustral complexes can be of three types: "(1) a complex constellated about the wish to reinstate the conditions similar to those prevailing before birth; (2) a complex that centres about the anxiety of insupport and helplessness; and (3) a complex that is anxiously directed against suffocation and confinement (anticlaustral tendency)" (Murray, 1938, p. 363).

Common trait. Allport's concept to account for the similarities among individuals stemming from the possession of a common human nature and a common culture. In the vast field of individual differences and uniqueness, common traits account for similarity. They have the character of convenient fictions, because they underestimate the uniqueness of persons.

Competence motivation. Robert White's term expressing the goal of effecting changes of the individual by the individual. It is intended in a broad biological sense to refer to an organism's capacity to interact effectually with its environment.

Complexes. Infantile or early childhood experiences determinative of later behavior. Murray defines it as: "An enduring integrate derived from one of the above-mentioned conditions that determines (unconsciously). The course of later development may be called a complex" (Murray, 1938, p. 363).

Conative abilities. Capacities of the ego referring to will power, conjunctivity of action, resolution of conflicts, selectivity in the impulses expressed and the social pressures responded to, initiative and self-sufficiency, responsibility for collective action, adherence to resolutions and agreements, and absence of psychopathological symptoms (Murray).

Convergence. A single course of action may actually reflect the operation of more than one disposition (Allport, 1961, p. 377).

Coping behavior. Motivated behavior, directed towards the achievement of ends. Compared with expressive behavior, coping is conscious, effortful, purposive, learned and often reactive (Maslow).

Creative needs. Needs aiming at the construction of new and useful thoughts and objects. Creative needs emphasize *adient tendencies* (Murray).

Deprivation motivation. Urges to strive for goal states, presently unachieved, that are necessary in order to ease the pain and discomfort caused by their absence. The aim of deprivation motivation is to decrease organismic tension and to restore homeostatic physiological balance (Maslow). *See* Lower needs.

Dynamic dispositions. *See* Personal disposition.

Effect needs. Needs marked by attempts to bring about a particular desired effect or goal which is extrinsic to the activity engaged in, that activity serving an instrumental purpose (Murray and Kluckhohn, 1956, p. 15).

Ego. As used by Murray, the word is an elaboration upon the Freudian usage; the rational and "differentiated governing establishment of personality," functioning to block and temper the expression of id impulses that are unacceptable to society and the superego through the employment of defenses. The ego is accorded an important, active role in determining the individual's functioning and in precipitating psychological growth. The ego includes capacities or abilities that are indispensable not only to adequate survival but also to excellence of living. These capacities or abilities are perceptual and apperceptual abilities, intellectual abilities, and conative abilities.

Ego ideal. A gradually developing, envisaged ideal seal which guides the ego, when that personality component becomes sufficiently differentiated and integrated, in arbitrating between emotional impulses from the id and superego imperatives (Murray and Kluckhohn, 1959, p. 28).

Esteem needs. *See* Need hierarchy.

Expressive behavior. Behavior that is an end in itself; "useless" in the sense of not being performed for some extrinsic end (Allport, though similar emphases are in Maslow and Murray).

Expressive traits. An individual's unique style of performing: Expressive traits give rise to *Areal, Extroversion-Introversion* and *Emphasis* factors (Allport).

Extroversion-Introversion factor. A factor derived in a cluster analysis of expressive moments, composed of such measures as overestimation of distance from the body, and underestimation of weights (Allport). *See* Areal factor; Factor of emphasis.

Factor of emphasis. A factor derived in a cluster analysis of expressive movement composed of such measures as voice intensity, movement during speech, writing pressure, and tapping pressure (Allport). *See* Areal factor; Extroversion-Introversion factor.

Functional autonomy. "Any acquired system of motivation in which the tensions involved are not of the same kind as the antecedent tensions from which the acquired system developed" (Allport, 1961, p. 229). Perseverative functional autonomy is less central and more the stuff of habit than is propriate functional autonomy.

Fusion. The operation of more than one need in a single course of action. Similar to Allport's concept of *convergence* (Murray, 1938, p. 86).

Growth motivation. Urgings to enrich living, to enlarge experience. Satisfaction has to do with realization of capabilities or ideals, through a process whereby the organism becomes more complex, differentiated, and potent. Growth motivation implies that satisfaction goes hand in hand with tension increase (Maslow). *See* Higher needs; Deprivation motivation.

Higher needs. Motivated behavior that expresses man's uniqueness and creative potential. Includes needs of *cognitive understanding* and *need for self actualization*. These higher needs represent *growth motivation*. The higher needs reflect biological potentialities rather than requirements, and do not insure physical survival, so much as to enrich life in psychological and social ways (Maslow).

Icarus complex. One form of urethal fixation characterized by a strong narcissism, cravings for immortality, and great aspirations that crumple in the face of failure (Murray). *See* Urethral complex.

Id. Murray's elaboration upon the original Freudian usage: The id, though still a repository of inner dynamic tendencies alone, contains not only the self-seeking, destructive impulses, but more acceptable tendencies as well, such as "respiration, ingestion of food, defecation, expressions of affection, endeavors to master the environment, and so forth. . . . The id is evidently the breeding ground of love and worship, as well as of the novel imaginations which are eventually applauded, instituted and cherished by society" (Murray and Kluckhohn, 1956, p. 24).

Idiographic laws. Derived from and applicable to the data of one individual, one case. A concept developed to explain that some behavior of one man would, strictly speaking, not be applicable to anyone else (Allport).

Instinctoid. Needs are not full-fledged instincts, but are instinctoid—because each need can be expressed and satisfied in many ways. There are no fixed action patterns. The instinctoid, or human, needs are less insistent and fixed than outright instincts, but share with them the property of arising from the complex whole that is the body. The individual's constitution, temperament, nervous system, and endocrine system, and all their capacities constitute the structure out of which needs emerge (Maslow, 1954, chapter 4). *See* Need, Maslow.

Intellectual abilities. Capacity of the ego referring to concentration and the conjunctivity and referentiality of thought and speech (Murray). *See* Ego, Murray.

Interchangeability. The characteristic of a syndrome whereby all parts of the syndrome are equivalent in having the same aim, and can therefore substitute for each other and have equal probability of appearance (Maslow). *See* Syndrome.

Internal proceedings. *See* Proceedings.

Lower needs. Motivated behavior that fulfills the biological requirement of the organism for physical survival, and does distinguish the human being from the other animals. Lower needs present *deprivation motivation,* and include physiological needs, safety needs, needs for belongingness and love, and esteem needs (Maslow). *See* Need hierarchy; Higher needs.

Mental needs. These needs do not have very specific goal states; they stem from the fact that "the human mind is inherently a transforming, creating, and representing organ; its function is to make symbols for things, to combine and recombine these symbols incessantly, and to communicate the most interesting of the combinations in a variety of languages, discursive (referential, scientific) and expressive (emotional, artistic)" (Murray and Kluckhohn, 1956, p. 16).

Metatheory. "Higher" theory, general orientation, attitudes, values beyond the specific propositions and statements constitutive of theory.

Morphogenic laws. Similar to idiographic laws, but with the *possible* applicability to more than one person (Allport).

Need for roleship. *See* Social-relational needs.

Need hierarchy. The hierarchical arrangement of sets of needs ranging from physiological needs, to safety needs, to needs for belongingness and love, to esteem needs, to need for cognitive understanding and need for self actualization. The nature of the interrelationship among these sets of needs is that those lower in the hierarchy must be satisfied to a substantial degree before those situated higher up can emerge strongly. The clear implication of Maslow's position is that the further up the hierarchy of needs one is able to go, the more individuality, humanity, and psychological health he will have. Physiological needs include such well-known requirements as for food, water, and air. Safety needs refer essentially to the avoidance of pain and physical damage through external forces. Needs for belongingness and love concern the general characteristic of living things to feel secure when in close, intimate contact with other organisms. Esteem needs refers to the importance of having status and acceptance in one's group. Need for cognitive understanding indicates that humans have an inborn push toward awareness, consciousness of themselves and of the external world, and an appreciation of meaning. Need for self-actualization refers to the natural tendency of the human to act in a manner expressive of his potentialities and capabilities, whatever they may be (Maslow).

Need-integrate. "A complex of one or more needs with the images that depict the common objects and actones associated with these tendencies." (Murray, 1938, p. 777).

Need. Murray's definition: "A construct (a convenient fiction or hypothetical concept) which stands for a force . . . in the brain region, a force which organizes perception, apperception, intellections, conation, and action in such a way as to transform in a certain direction an existing, unsatisfying situation. A need is sometimes provoked directly by internal processes of a certain kind . . . but, more frequently (when in a state of readiness), by the occurrence of one of a few commonly effective press" (Murray, 1938, p. 123–24).

n Abasement	n Infavoidance
n Achievement	n Inviolacy
n Acquisition	n Noxavoidance
n Activity	n Nurturance
n Affiliation	n Order
n Aggression	n Passivity
n Autonomy	n Play
n Blamavoidance	n Recognition
n Cognizance	n Rejection
n Construction	n Retention
n Counteraction	n Seclusion
n Defendence	n Sentience
n Deference	n Sex
n Dominance	n Similance
n Exhibition	n Succorance
n Exposition	n Superiority
n Harmavoidance	n Understanding

See Activity needs; Creative needs; Effect needs; Mental
  needs; Social-relational needs; Viserogenic needs.
Negative needs. Needs that find expression in the avoidance
  or termination of noxious, unpleasant conditions. Behavior
  that restores physiological balance—for example, drinking
  to quench thirst—reflect negative needs (Murray).
Peak experience. An intense, often mystical experience that
  can radically change an individual. Personal revelations of
  angels, deities, and associated epiphanal phenomena might
  exemplify one sort of peak experience. "The feeling of great
  ecstasy, wonder and awe, the loss of placing in time and
  space with, finally, the conviction that something extremely
  important and valuable has happened" (Maslow, 1962,
  p. 97).
Personal disposition. "A generalized neuropsychic structure
  (peculiar to the individual), with the capacity to render
  many stimuli functionally equivalent, and to initiate and
  guide consistent (equivalent) forms of adaptive and stylistic behavior" (Allport, 1961, p. 373).
Propotent needs. The degree to which a need takes precedence over others when it is aroused. Maslow assumes that
  the lower a need on the need hierarchy the greater its
  propotency.
Proceedings. Data units that apply to Murray's conception of
  personality. A proceeding can be very roughly identified as
  the initiation and completion of a "dynamically significant
  pattern of behavior," that involves real or imagined interaction between the subject and an animate or inanimate
  aspect of his environment. *External proceedings* are real—
  such as the reading of this glossary. *Internal Proceedings*
  are imagined—such as the seduction of a daydream.
Proactive functioning. Self-initiated behavior, distinguished
  from reactive functioning, or a passive, responsive attitude
  to external stimulation (Allport; but Maslow and Murray
  also agree).
Process needs. Related to process activity defined as "spon-

taneous, random, ungoverned but yet expressive caco-
phonies of energy, process needs are engaged in for their
inherent, intrinsic pleasure" (Murray, 1954, p. 448).

Propriate functional autonomy. *See* Functional autonomy.

Propriate functioning. Where thoughts, feelings, and actions
seem subjectively chosen and hence express the self (Allport).

Propriate striving. Similar to Maslow's and Murray's concepts,
Allport's term refers to the "directedness" or "intention-
ality" that the course of a person's life may demonstrate.
Also refers to the "ownness" or phenomenal closeness of
the person's directional activities.

Proprium (or self). The superordinate concept in Allport's
system, which serves an organizing and integrating role and
provides an impetus to psychological growth. The functions of the proprium are sense of body, self-identity, self-
esteem, self-extension, rational coping, self image, and propriate striving. The concept of proprium parallels the concept of ego (Allport, 1961, p. 110–38).

Reactive functioning. *See* Proactive functioning.

Safety needs. *See* Need hierarchy.

Schedules. Arrangements for the orderly expression of contiguously aroused needs. Through ego functioning, schedules come about (Murray, 1956, p. 38–39).

Secondary dispositions. Personal dispositions of relatively
transient importance (Allport). *See* Cardinal dispositions;
Central dispositions; Personal dispositions.

Self-actualizing personality. The common features, or traits,
of the person who has successfully transcended the survival needs and is leading a life expressive of self-actualization and cognitive understanding are: (1) realistic orientation, or the ability to see self and world accurately, (2) acceptance of self, others, and the natural world; (3) spontaneity, or the ability to experience and implement one's
reactions straightforwardly; (4) task orientation rather

than self-preoccupation; (5) sense of privacy; (6) independence; (7) vivid appreciativeness; (8) spirituality that is not necessarily religious in a formal sense; (9) sense of identity with mankind; (10) feelings of intimacy with a few loved ones; (11) democratic values; (12) recognition of the difference between means and ends; (13) humor that is philosophical rather than hostile; (14) creativity; (15) non-conformism (Maslow).

Serial. "A directionally organized intermittent succession of proceedings. . . . Thus, a serial (such as a friendship, a marriage, a career in business) is a relatively long functional unit which can be formulated only roughly" (Murray, 1951a, p. 272).

Serial programs. Arrangements that insure a gradual movement of the individual toward the achievement of complex goals. Serial programs come about through the capacities or functions of the ego (Murray).

Socio-relational needs. These needs arise from the inherently social nature of man and include such specific dispositions as the need for roleship—the need "to become and to remain an accepted and respected, differentiated and integrated part of a congenial, functioning group, the collective purposes of which are congruent with the individual's needs" (Murray, 1954, p. 451–52).

Subsidiation. The process by which less potent needs can become instrumental to the satisfaction of other needs (Murray, 1938, p. 86–88).

Superego. The internal representation of the value system of an individual's society, in terms of which he judges and disciplines himself and others. Murray has elaborated upon the concept as used by Freud by recognizing the determining influences of such extra-parental factors as peer group pressures, literature, and the like (Murray).

Syndrome. A complex of symptoms or parts of behavior that are usually found to occur together, given a unifying name;

a general concept that refers to a type of organization, namely an interdependent organized group of symptoms. Particular organizations of personality that make a person just who he is, and his life just what it is. Syndromes are the organized whole of the interrelationship and mutual influences of the needs characteristic of a person. Syndromes exhibit such characteristics as: (1) interchangeability, (2) circular determination, (3) the tendency to resist change, re-establish itself after change, and to change as a whole (Maslow, 1954, p. 31–36, 37–61).

Thema. A combination of a need and a press; themas determine proceedings (Murray).

Uniqueness principle. Individual differences in gratification history implies that each person will have an idiosyncratic set of requirements that must be fulfilled before he can grow closer toward self-actualization (Maslow).

Unity thema. A need-press combination that is pervasive, having been formed early in the individual's life (Murray, 1938, pp. 604–605).

Urethral complex. Murray is unusual in the amount of emphasis he puts on the urethral complexes. In his early writings he tended to include here bedwetting and urethral eroticism, with little further elaboration. But more recently he has given special importance to urethral fixations in understanding the competitiveness and ambition rampant in American society. One form of urethral fixation is the Icarus complex (Murray, 1938).

Value-Vector. The vector principle refers to the nature of the directionality shown by behavior (for example, rejection, acquisition, construction). The value principle refers to the ideals that are important to people (for example, knowledge, beauty, authority). A value-vector matrix is compiled in diagnosing what each person believes is worthwhile and the particular ways in which he moves to make these beliefs actualities (Murray).

Viserogenic needs. Needs stemming from tissue requirements, having very specific, easily recognized goals (for example, need for food, warmth, sleep). Similar to physiological needs (Maslow), and opportunistic striving (Allport). Also Murray.

Bibliography

Allport, G. W. The radio as a stimulus situation. *Acta Psychologica*, 1935, 1–6.

Allport, G. W. *Personality: A psychological interpretation.* New York: Henry Holt & Company, 1937.

Allport, G. W. *The use of personal documents in psychological research.* New York: Social Science Research Council, 1942.

Allport, G. W. The trend in motivational theory, *American Journal of Orthopsychiatry*, 1953, 23, 107–19.

Allport, G. W. *Becoming: Basic considerations for a psychology of personality.* New Haven: Yale University Press, 1955.

Allport, G. W. Open system and personality theory, *Journal of Abnormal and Social Psychology*, 1960, 61, 301–310. (a)

Allport, G. W. *Personality and social encounter.* Boston: Beacon Press, 1960. (b)

Allport, G. W. *Pattern and growth in personality.* New York: Holt, Rinehart and Winston, 1961.

Allport, G. W. The general and the unique in psychological science, *Journal of Personality*, 1962, 30, 405–22.

Allport, G. W. Behavioral science, religion, and mental health, *Journal of Religion and Health,* 1963, 2, 187–97.

Allport, G. W. Traits revisited, in J. T. Flynn and H. T. Gorler (eds.), *Assessing behavior.* Reading, Mass.: Addison-Wesley Publishing Company, 1967.

Allport, G. W. Personality: Contemporary viewpoints (I), in D. L. Sills (ed.), *International Encyclopedia of the Social Sciences,* Vol. 12, pp. 1–5. New York: The MacMillan Company and The Free Press, 1968. (a)

Allport, G. W. *The person in psychology.* Boston: Beacon, 1968. (b)

Allport, G. W., and F. H. Allport. *A-S reaction study.* Boston: Houghton Mifflin Company, 1928.

Allport, G. W., J. S. Bruner, and E. M. Jandorf. Personality under social catastrophe: Ninety life histories of the Nazi revolution. *Character and Personality,* 1941, 10, 1–22.

Allport, G. W., and H. Cantrill. Judging personality from voice, *Journal of Social Psychology,* 1934, 5, 37–55.

Allport, G. W., and H. S. Odbert. Trait-names: A psycho-lexical study, *Psychological Monographs,* 1936, 47, No. 211, 1–171.

Allport, G. W., and L. Postman. An analysis of rumor. *Public Opinion Quarterly,* 1947, 10, 501–17.

Allport, G. W., and P. E. Vernon. A test for personal values. *Journal of Abnormal and Social Psychology,* 1931, 25, 268–372.

Allport, G. W., and P. E. Vernon. *Studies in expressive movement.* New York: The MacMillan Company, 1933.

Allport, G. W., P. E. Vernon, and G. Lindzey. *A study of values* (2d ed.). Boston: Houghton Mifflin Company, 1951.

Argyle, M. *Religious behavior.* Glencoe, Ill.: The Free Press, 1960.

Atkinson, J. W. (ed.) *Motives in fantasy, action, and society.* Princeton: Van Nostrand Company, 1958.

Baldwin, A. L. Personal structure analysis: A statistical method for investigating the single personality, *Journal of Abnormal and Social Psychology*, 1940, 37, 163–83.

Bernadin, A. C., and R. Jessor. A construct validation of the Edwards Personal Preference Schedule with respect to dependency, *Journal of Consulting Psychology*, 1957, 21, 63–67.

Bolles, R. C. The usefulness of the drive concept, in M. R. Jones (ed.), *Nebraska Symposium on Motivation*. Lincoln: University of Nebraska Press, 1958.

Braun, J., and P. Asta. Intercorrelations between the Personal Orientation Inventory and the Gordon Personal Inventory Scores, *Psychological Reports*, 1968, 23, 1197–98.

Braun, J., and D. LeFaro. A further study of the fakability of the Personal Orientation Inventory, *Journal of Clinical Psychology*, 1969, 25, 296–99.

Bugental, J. (ed.) *Challenges of humanistic psychology*. New York: McGraw-Hill, 1967.

Byrd, R. E. Training in a non-group, *Journal of Humanistic Psychology*, 1967, 7, 18–27.

Centers, R. Motivational aspects of occupational stratification, *Journal of Social Psychology*, 1948, 28, 187–217.

Culbert, S. A., J. V. Clark, and H. K. Bobele. Measures of change toward self actualization in two sensitivity training groups, *Journal of Counseling Psychology*, 1968, 15, 53–57.

Dandes, M. Psychological health and teaching effectiveness, *Journal of Teacher Education*, 1966, 17, 301–306.

Davis, W. A. The motivation of the underprivileged worker, in W. F. Whyte (ed.), *Industry and society*, pp. 84–106. New York: McGraw-Hill, 1946.

deCharms, R., H. W. Morrison, W. Reitman, and D. C. McClelland. Behavioral correlates of directly and indirectly measured achievement motivation, in D. C. McClelland (ed.), *Studies in motivation.* New York: Appleton-Century-Crofts, 1955.

Edwards, A. L. *Edwards Personal Preference Schedule.* New York: Psychological Corporation, 1963.

Estes, S. G. Judging personality from expressive behavior, *Journal of Abnormal and Social Psychology,* 1938, 33, 217–36.

Fisher, G. Performance of psychopathic felons on a measure of self actualization, *Educational and Psychological Measurement,* 1968, 28, 561–63.

Fiske, D. W. The inherent variability of behavior, in D. W. Fiske and S. R. Maddi (eds.), *Functions of varied experience.* Homewood, Ill.: Dorsey Press, 1961.

Fiske, D. W. Problems in measuring personality, in J. M. Wepman and R. W. Heine (eds.), *Concepts of personality.* Chicago: Aldine Publishing Company, 1963.

Fiske, D. W., and S. R. Maddi (eds.), *Functions of varied experience.* Homewood, Ill.: Dorsey Press, 1961.

Foulds, M. L. Self actualization and the communication of facilitative conditions under counseling, *Journal of Counseling Psychology,* 1969, 16, 132–36.

Fox, J., R. Knapp, and W. Michael. Assessment of self-actualization of psychiatric patients: Validity of the Personal Orientation Inventory, *Educational and Psychological Measurement,* 1968, 28, 565–69.

Graff, R., and H. Bradshaw. Relationship of a measure of self-actualization to dormitory assistant effectiveness, *Journal of Counseling Psychology,* 1970, 17, 502–505.

Grossack, M., T. Armstrong, and G. Lussieu. Correlates of self-actualization, *Journal of Humanistic Psychology,* 1966, 37.

Guinan, J., and M. Foulds. Marathan group: Facilitator of personal growth? *Journal of Humanistic Psychology,* 1970, 17, 145–49.

Hall, C. S., and G. Lindzey. *Theories of personality.* New York: John Wiley & Sons, 1957.

Hall, D. T., and K. E. Nougaim. An examination of Maslow's need hierarchy in an organizational setting, *Organizational Behavior and Human Performance,* 1968, 3, 12–35.

Huntley, C. W. Judgments of self based upon records of expressive behavior, *Journal of Abnormal and Social Psychology,* 1940, 35, 398–427.

Ilardi, R., and W. May. A reliability study of Shostrom's Personal Orientation Inventory, *Journal of Humanistic Psychology,* 1968, 8, 68–72.

Jackson, D. *Personality Research Form.* Goshen, N. Y.: Research Psychologists Press, 1967.

Kelly, G. A. *The psychology of personal constructs.* New York: W. W. Norton & Company, 1955.

Kilpatrick, F. P., and H. Cantril. Self-anchoring scale: A measure of the individual's unique reality world, *Journal of Individual Psychology,* 1960, 16, 158–70.

Klavetter, R., and R. Mogar. Stability and internal consistency of a measure of self-actualization, *Psychological Reports,* 1967, 21, 422–24.

Knapp, R. Relationship of a measure of self-actualization to neuroticism and extraversion, *Journal of Consulting Psychology,* 1965, 29, 168–72.

LeMay, M., and V. Damm. The Personal Orientation Inventory as a measure of self-actualization of underachievers, *Measurement and Evaluation in Guidance,* 1968, 110–14.

Lyman, E. Occupational differences in the value attached to work, *American Journal of Sociology,* 1955, 61, 138–44.

McClain, E. Further validation of the Personal Orientation Inventory: Assessment of the self-actualization of school counselors, *Journal of Consulting and Clinical Psychology,* 1970, 35, 21–22.

McClelland, D. C. *Personality.* New York: Dryden Press, 1951.

McClelland, D. C. Methods of measuring human motivation, in J. W. Atkinson (ed.), *Motives in fantasy, action, and society*. Princeton: D. Van Nostrand Company, 1958.

McClelland, D. C. *The achieving society*. Princeton: D. Van Nostrand Company, 1961.

McClelland, D. C., J. W. Atkinson, R. A. Clark, and E. L. Lowell. *The achievement motive*. New York: Appleton-Century-Crofts, 1953.

MacKinnon, D. W. Personality and the realization of creative potential, *American Psychologist*, 1965, 20, 273–81.

Maddi, S. R. *Personality theories: A comparative analysis*. Homewood, Ill.: Dorsey Press, 1968.

Mandler, G., and W. Kessen. *The language of psychology*. New York: John Wiley & Sons, 1959.

Maslow, A. H. The role of dominance in the social and sexual behavior of infra-human primates: III. A theory of sexual behavior of infra-human primates, *Journal of Genetic Psychology*, 1936, 48, 310–38.

Maslow, A. H. The influence of familiarization on preference, *Journal of Experimental Psychology*, 1937, 15, 487–90.

Maslow, A. H. Dominance-feeling, personality, and social behavior in women, *Journal of Social Psychology*, 1939, 10, 3–39.

Maslow, A. H. Self-esteem (dominance-feeling) and sexuality in women, *Journal of Social Psychology*, 1942, 16, 259–94.

Maslow, A. H. Self-actualizing people: A study of psychological health, also in W. Wolfl (ed.), *Values in personality research*. New York: Grune & Stratton, 1950.

Maslow, A. H. Higher needs and personality, *Dialectica*, 1951, 5, 257–65.

Maslow, A. H. *Motivation and personality*. New York: Harper & Brothers, 1954.

Maslow, A. H. Deficiency motivation and growth motivation, in M. R. Jones (ed.), *Nebraska Symposium on Motivation*. Lincoln: University of Nebraska Press, 1955.

Maslow, A. H. Defense and growth, *Merrill-Palmer Quarterly,* 1956, 3, 36–47.

Maslow, A. H. A philosophy of psychology, in J. Fairchild (ed.), *Personal problems and psychological frontiers.* New York: Sheridan House, 1956.

Maslow, A. H. Eupsychia, the good society, *Journal of Humanistic Psychology,* 1961, 1, 1–11.

Maslow, A. H. *Toward a psychology of being.* Princeton: D. Van Nostrand Company, 1962.

Maslow, A. H. Criteria for judging needs to be instinctoid, in M. R. Jones (ed.), *Human motivation: A symposium.* Lincoln: University of Nebraska Press, 1964. (a)

Maslow, A. H. Synergy in the society and in the individual, *Journal of Individual Psychology,* 1964, 20, 153–64. (b)

Maslow, A. H. *Religions, values and peak-experiences.* Columbus: Ohio State University Press, 1964. (c)

Maslow, A. H. *Eupsychian management: A journal.* Homewood, Ill.: Richard D. Irwin, 1965.

Maslow, A. H. *The psychology of science: A reconnaissance.* New York: Harper & Row Publishers, 1966.

Maslow, A. H. Self-actualization and beyond, in J. Bugental (ed.), *Challenges of humanistic psychology.* New York: McGraw-Hill, 1967. (a)

Maslow, A. H. A theory of meta-motivation: The biological rooting of the value-life, *Journal of Humanistic Psychology,* 1967, 2, 93–127. (b)

Maslow, A. H. *Toward a psychology of being.* (2d ed.). Princeton: D. Van Nostrand Company, 1968. (a)

Maslow, A. H. Some educational implications of the humanistic psychologies, *Harvard Educational Review,* Fall, 1968, 38, No. 4. (b)

Maslow, A. H. A conversation with Abraham H. Maslow, *Psychology Today,* 1968, 2, No. 2, 35 ff. (c)

Maslow, A. H., and N. L. Mintz. Effects of esthetic surroundings: I. Initial effects of three esthetic conditions upon perceiving "energy" and "well-being" in faces, *Journal of Psychology*, 1956, 41, 247–54.

Maslow, A. H., and B. Mittelman. *Principles of Abnormal Psychology*. New York: Harper & Row, 1941.

Maslow, A. H., and I. Szilagyi-Kessler. Security and breast feeding, *Journal of Abnormal and Social Psychology*, 1946, 41, 83–85.

Morgan, C. D., and H. A. Murray. A method of investigating fantasies, *Archives of Neurology and Psychiatry*, American Medical Asso. *Chicago*, 1935, 4, 310–29.

Morse, N., and R. Weiss. The function and meaning of work and the job, *American Sociological Review*, 1955, 20, 191–98.

Murray, H. A. The effect of fear upon estimates of the maliciousness of other personalities, *Journal of Social Psychology*, 1933, 4, 310–29.

Murray, H. A. *Explorations in personality: A clinical and experimental study of fifty men of college age*. New York: Oxford University Press, 1938.

Murray, H. A. What should psychologists do about psychoanalysis, *Journal of Abnormal and Social Psychology*, 1940, 35, 150–75.

Murray, H. A. Problems in clinical research: Round table, *American Journal of Ortho-Psychiatry*, 1947, 17, 203–210.

Murray, H. A. Research planning: A few proposals, in S. S. Sargeant (ed.), *Culture and personality*, pp. 195–212. New York: Viking Fund, 1949.

Murray, H. A. Some basic psychological assumptions and conceptions, *Dialectica*, 1951, 5, 266–92. (a)

Murray, H. A. In nomine diaboli, *New England Quarterly*, 1951, 24, 435–52. (b)

Murray, H. A. Toward a classification of interaction, in T. Parsons and E. A. Shils (eds.), *Toward a general theory of action*. Cambridge: Harvard University Press, 1954.

Murray, H. A. American Icarus. In A. Burton, and R. E. Harris (eds.), *Clinical Studies of Personality*, Vol. 2. New York: Harper, 1955.

Murray, H. A. Preparations for the scaffold of a comprehensive system, in S. Koch (ed.), *Psychology: A study of a science*, Vol. 3. New York: McGraw-Hill, 1959.

Murray, H. A. Prospect for psychology, *Science*, 1962, 136, No. 3515, 483–88.

Murray, H. A. Studies of stressful interpersonal disputations, *American Psychologist*, 1963, 18, 28–36.

Murray, H. A. Autobiography. In E. G. Boring & G. Lindzey, (eds.), *History of psychology in autobiography*, Vol. V, pp. 258–310. New York: Appleton-Century-Crofts, 1967.

Murray, H. A. Personality: Contemporary viewpoints (II), in David L. Sills (ed.), *International Encyclopedia of the Social Sciences*, Vol. 12, pp. 5–13. New York: The Mac-Millan Company and The Free Press, 1968.

Murray, H. A., and C. Kluckhohn. Outline of a conception of personality, in C. Kluckhohn, H. A. Murray, and D. M. Schneider (eds.), *Personality in nature, society, and culture*, (2d Ed.). New York: Alfred A. Knopf, 1956.

Murray, H. A., and C. D. Morgan. A clinical study of sentiments, *Genetic Psychology Monographs*, 1945, 32, 3–311.

Murray, H. A., and D. R. Wheeler. A note on the possible clairvoyance of dreams, *Journal of Psychology*, 1936, 3, 309–13.

Office of Strategic Services Assessment Staff. *Assessment of men*. New York: Rinehart & Company, 1948.

Paige, J. M. Letters from Jenny: An approach to the clinical analysis of personality structure by computer, in P. J. Stone (ed.), *The general inquirer: A computer approach to content analysis*. Cambridge: M.I.T. Press, 1966.

Pellegrin, R., and C. Coates. Executives and supervisors; Contrasting definitions of career success, *Administrative Science Quarterly*, 1957, 1, 506–17.

Pettigrew, T. F. *Profile of the Negro American.* Princeton, New Jersey: D. Van Nostrand, 1964.

Porter, L. Job attitudes in management: II. Perceived importance of needs as a function of job level, *Journal of Applied Psychology,* 1963, 47, 141–48.

Rotter, J. B. Generalized expectancies for internal versus external control of reinforcement, *Psychological Monographs,* 1966, 80, Whole No. 609.

Rotter, J. B., M. Seeman, and S. Liverant. Internal versus external control of reinforcements: A major variable in behavior theory, in N. F. Washburne (ed.), *Decisions, values, and groups,* Vol. 2, pp. 473–516. London: Pergamon Press, 1962.

Shapiro, M. B. The single case in fundamental clinical psychological research, *British Journal of Medical Psychology,* 1961, 34, 255–62.

Shostrom, E. An inventory for the measurement of self-actualization, *Educational and Psychological Measurement,* 1965, 24, 207–18.

Shostrom, E. *Manual for the Personal Orientation Inventory (POI): An inventory for the measurement of self-actualization.* San Diego: Educational and Industrial Testing Service, 1966.

Shostrom, E., and R. Knapp. The relationship of a measure of self-actualization (POI) to a measure of pathology (MMPI) and to therapeutic growth, *American Journal of Psychotherapy,* 1966, 20, 193–202.

Skinner, B. F. Are theories of learning necessary? *Psychological Review,* 1950, 57, 193–216.

Stein, M. I. Explorations in typology, in R. W. White (ed.), *The study of lives.* New York: Atherton Press, 1963.

Stephenson, W. *The study of behavior: Q-technique and its methodology.* Chicago: The University of Chicago Press, 1953.

Stern, G. G. *Preliminary manual: Activities index—college*

characteristics index. Syracuse, N. Y.: Syracuse University Psychological Research Center, 1958. (a)

Stern, G. G. *Preliminary record: Activities index—college characteristics index.* Syracuse, N. Y.: Syracuse University Psychological Research Center, 1958. (b)

Stewart, R. A. C. Academic performance and components of self-actualization, *Perceptual and Motor Skills,* 1968, 26, 918.

Veroff, J., J. Atkinson, S. Feld, and G. Gurin. The use of thematic apperception to assess motivation in a nationwide interview study, *Psychological Monographs,* 1960, 74, Whole No. 499.

White, R. W. Motivation reconsidered: The concept of competence, *Psychological Review,* 1959, 66, 297–333.

Wilson, W. C. Extrinsic religious values and prejudice. *Journal of Abnormal and Social Psychology,* 1960, 60, 286–88.

Name Index

Subject Index